COLLECTED WRITINGS
FROM
THE STORYBOOK HOUSE

FIFTH AVENUE WRITERS

David Baker   Elizabeth Rodenz

Sarah Moreno   Sarah Holler

Carole Shimko   Joanne Wright

© 2022, David Baker, Sarah Holler, Sarah Moreno, Elizabeth Rodenz, Carole Shimko, Joanne Wright.
Fifth Avenue Writers
5935 5th Avenue, Pittsburgh, PA 15232

Printed and published in
the United States of America 2022
10 9 8 7 6 5 4 3 2 1

ISBN: 978-1-68564-281-5

Please direct all inquiries to the address above

Library of Congress Control Number: 2021922158

Library of Congress Cataloging-in-Publication Data:

Fifth Avenue Writers
1. anthology 2. collected writings 3. short stories 4. poetry
5. memoir 6. Memoir vignettes.
2022

Table of Contents

Fifth Avenue Writers vii

Joanne Wright 1

Jazz 4

Cherry and Elm(er) 6

George and Me 7

The Vixen's Tail 19

Sicilian Postcards 29

David Baker 43

An Era Lost 46

Upon the Face of This Earth 50

Searching 51

Coming Late 53

Tradition 55

The Story of Granddad Hibbitt 56

Ice Cream 59

Is Mankind Born Evil? 61

Walter 63

Sarah Moreno 69

Summer Night in the 50s 72

The Fat Girl 74

Sugar Cookies 78

Sorrow 79

Elizabeth Rodenz 83

Two Hearts 86

Gifts Given 87

Women Rise Up 88

The Year of Loss 90

Travel to the Edge 91

Seasons Reign 92

The Magic of Three 95

Mr. Penny 96

Carole Shimko 107

Ode to the HOA 110

Broken Cookies 114

Mother of the Gloom 122

The Bride Answers Back 123

The Reluctant Poet 124

A Room with a Pew 125

Sarah Holler 129

Enjoying the Cruise 132

Senses of Majorca 133

Winter Quiet 134

Missing Teeth 135

First Encounter 142

Epilogue 145

Fifth Avenue Writers

Writing is a solitary act. The writer sits with a blank page with thoughts swirling around. The words finally appear. The page is ripped up or crumbled, discarded. The delete key is in over-drive. A few sentences are scribbled on pieces of paper or in a journal, moved from here to there, lost for years, decades, resurfacing now and then. Along the way, life got in the way.

The longing to write is still there, but paralysis has set in. Thoughts that might resonate with others are put on the shelf. Words that you must write are forgotten or a faded memory. Then one day something triggers that desire again, maybe a life-changing event or maybe just saying, "I must write." You realize those words ring so true, and you will answer the call.

Then you come together with other writers in a safe haven. That is what we were fortunate enough to find at a charming home on Fifth Avenue. It is a home such as might be imagined in childhood dreams with its many rooms, nooks, and crannies. In this special place, our writing group meets once a week, providing inspiration and encouragement to all. When the weather allows, we gather in the backyard garden with birds, squirrels, flowers, and herbs.

Clocks of all ages, shapes, and sizes toll the passing hours as we, the authors, share our writings surrounded by treasures from around the world and three adorable, affectionate beagles. It is our Storybook House.

Initially, we started out wanting to write and hone our craft. We soon found contentment and joy in writing and supporting our fellow writers. Along the way, we realized our writings needed to have a home, not be put on the shelf, shoved in a drawer, lost for now, forever.

This collection of writings is meant to share with you, the reader, expressions of some of our intimate thoughts and longings, love and sorrow, humor, wonder, and the paths we have traveled. We are an eclectic group with various life experiences, evidenced by our writings, which are as different as we are. Just peek at the titles in the table of contents.

We hope you will sit with us for a little while.

Joanne Wright

Jazz

Cherry and Elm(er)

George and Me

The Vixen's Tail

Sicilian Postcards

I have journaled most of my life. I keep a notebook next to my bed, ready to use when my thoughts or feelings swell up and need to spill out. I've used journals to work through grief and fear and to express gratitude. I record significant events and write about new things I've learned. I ponder existential questions and capture my dreams. In my journals, I jot down spontaneous ideas for a poem or story to come back to later, and I make note of revisions that insist on being noticed in the middle of the night. Writing calms me, makes me joyous, helps me gain clarity, and seals new information into my brain.

I am an analytical thinker. In my professional life, creativity has taken the form of problem-solving, planning and organizing, designing for product development, and testing. Writing creative fiction involves many of the same skills – defining a plot with conflicts to be resolved, planning a sequence of events that will keep the reader engaged, designing and developing complex characters, and editing and rewriting until the piece is as I had intended. Writing creative fiction is an outlet for my analytical nature.

I am a lover of music of all forms, particularly world music, jazz, classical, folk, and some technical, punk, rap, and pop. Poetry is music with words, structures, and rhythms that work together to bring forth feelings, thoughts, story, and song. Topics are limitless. Poetic themes can include philosophical musings, social activist outcry, lyrics of longing for a new or lost love, an expression of reverence for nature, or commentary on little-noticed elements of day-to-day life. Poetry is a composition in words, with images that tug at the emotions and sounds that speak the language of the soul. Writing poetry is an instrument for airing my love of music.

I have been published in a technical journal and quoted in a non-profit organization's Christmas card. I've contributed to published recipe books and newsletters. Writing a memoir in poetry for family history purposes is my current work-in-progress.

Similar to journaling, I have found that creative writing can be both meditative and outward-looking. It has often increased my understanding of self and my empathy for fellow humans. Writing makes me consider different perspectives. It drives me to research and to learn something new about the world. In that sense, writing makes me feel more fully alive.

Jazz

Shimmering brass horns
Harmonize
Come and go in parted measures
Clouds of chords materialize
Bass riffs, key shifts
Improvise
Scat away the jumpy jitters

Remember those days
When love was all you thought about
You'd get through the workday
But all you wanted was love
Lived for it
After work happy hours
Being out, seeking out ...

Each to each, play tight and listen
Slow down straighten, cry blues hasten
Sling hash clash clink
Mish and mash drink
Tall chill solo, swing jive take five
Anesthetize, rhapsodize
Synch

Well, babe, we found our overture
Like one celestial chord, we jammed
Tapped the beat, felt the heat
Kept each other on key
We slammed through variations, and now,
We know … Souls…
Come and go in parted measures

Oh, we had our spin sublime
Set in motion for the first time when
Tyche and Euterpe
Took the floor and, with a wink
Fused a link, fortune and music, you and me
We … yes, we … we sure … we surely did
Synch

White light blips on black wingtips
Slides and slips
Dives and dips

Cherry and Elm(er)

Slender, she rose, eighty years in her place.
Companion as old and noble stood west.
From birth, side by side, they grew breast to chest,
Played ticklish games, counted stars, reached for space.

At sixty, his height began to outpace.
Stirrings fluttered, so close to her loveliness.
Swaying together, he chanced a caress.
Graceful curves rustled a blush to his face.

In twenty new springs, he witnessed her worth –
White-flowered nectar, dry butterfly dock,
Black fruit for blue-jays, woodpecker door knock,
Warmth of her roots, under frozen, cracked earth.

Life's current swept 'way in one night's downpour.
In disbelief, she, Sweet Chérie, could not speak.
He reached to catch her, too late and too weak
As river beneath seeped into her core.

For no fault of his, though blame he assumed –
T'was his to protect the lady, his realm.
Body felled, as in life, would still overwhelm.
Bowed low, Elm(er) withered while grief consumed.

Sunshine unfiltered burned into scarred wood.
Should she come again, to the ground, he would bend
To hold up his missed and beloved friend.
Dew gleamed. In the clearing, a sapling stood.

George and Me

There was a boy once … at the mall … in the elevator. He was standing against the back wall after everyone but me got off on two. He barely came up to my hip and had these chubby baby cheeks, so … Well, I don't know kids, but I took him to be about three, four years old.

When I saw him there alone, I knew he was lost. The elevator door was closing, and I stuck my foot out to stop it. I stepped halfway out into the hallway, looking for his parents. The door kept pressing against my back, and a bell was dinging. The hallway was empty. I turned back into the elevator and looked at the boy. His blond hair half-covered his eyes, and it was touching the top of his shirt collar. He was a dirty little thing – had on a gray shirt with what-used-to-be-white stripes, blue shorts, and sneakers with untied, ragged shoelaces. His knees were smudged. I said hello, but he stared straight ahead and didn't look at me.

When the elevator announced three, (one of those talking elevators – you know the kind I mean), the doors opened, and the boy stepped out. There was no one else in the hallway. "Wait a minute!" I reached for his arm and tugged him back. "Let's see if your Mum and Dad are looking for you." Maybe he'd ducked in on the first floor, and the nasty door closed before Mum could get the kids organized.

We got to one, and a couple of teenagers and a man stepped in. They reached in front of me to push the buttons for their floors. No Mum waiting. Back up to three. The boy and I got off, but I grabbed his arm before he could race off. I bent down so our faces were level. He pulled his arm away from my grip. "Do you know where your parents are, sweetie? I'll take you to them, but I don't know where they are." He looked at the floor. "Can you tell me your name?" I wasn't sure if he could hear me, just staring at the floor like that.

Should I go to Security? They must have a Security office somewhere in this mall.

Just then, the boy threw his arms around my neck and pulled his legs up to hug my waist. I staggered, though he was light. I was afraid I was going to fall head-first to the floor on top of him. Somehow, I caught my balance and, with some effort, I straightened up. You know what he did next? He put his head on my shoulder. I couldn't help it – I hugged his warm little body to my chest. What a sweet thing!

Well, the hair salon was on the third floor, and I was already late for my appointment and really needed the cut. When I got to the counter, I put the boy down but took his hand and held it tight. It wouldn't take long to get my haircut, and I could skip the blow-dry. I thought I'd hear an announcement on the PA system that a boy was lost. We'd look for the Security office as soon as we were done.

The receptionist gave the boy a lollipop. I told her his name was George. "A big name for such a little one," she said. The stylist made a fuss over the boy – put him on a booster seat in the chair next to mine and spun him around. His eyes got big. I think he liked it. He stared at himself in the mirror, moving his head from side to side, studying his face like it was the first time he'd ever seen it. Serious the whole time. The name I'd given him is serious too, so it suited him.

That hair, though! I asked, "How about a trim for George too?"

———

Back in the elevator, I was still listening for the announcement. There was none. I wondered if the PA system reached the hair salon and if it came through on the elevator. We got off on one. I held George's hand, tightly again, as we walked down one corridor, then up the other. I looked down each side-hallway where they usually have the administration offices and restrooms, searching for a sign for the Security office, but no luck.

When we came to the Disney store, George pulled my hand and dragged me inside. The young woman behind the counter watched us and looked annoyed. She was squinting her eyes at us and shaking her head like she was saying, "you'd better not." George raced to the shelf with the Toy Story figures. He knew just where they were. He played a make-believe game with the figures, facing them toward one another and rocking them back and forth like they were having a conversation. He didn't make a sound, though. When he got tired of the game, he moved to the Pixar cars. Then it was me who tugged at George's arm to go back to the mall.

A security guard was standing beside the entrance to Hilley's Department Store. As we approached, he stared at George. He still had his eyes on the boy when I asked him to point us in the direction of the Security office. He hesitated before answering.

So, the conversation went something like this, as I remember.

"Are you the boy's mother?"

I stiffened at that. "Well, no, I think he's lost – he was alone on the elevator and that's why I'm looking for the Security Office."

Under his breath, "Well, that's the second time this week."

What was that? "So you know him?" I asked.

The officer squatted down in front of the boy. "Yeah, we know each other, don't we, son? Looks like you got yourself a haircut." He stood back up to look at me again. "Yeah, this is the second time this week that someone brought him in. No one claimed him last time, so we had to call Children and Youth Services. They came to pick him up and when they saw him, said they knew who he belonged to. Not the first time for them either. Must've returned him to his folks." He raised his fingers to his lips and mimicked drinking from a bottle. "And now he's back." He shook his head. "This time it'll be foster care, I'm afraid."

I let this sink in and appreciated his being so talkative. I noted the name on his badge. *Grant Peasely*, it said. I couldn't help but notice his blue eyes, which were so pale they were ghostly. But he had a nice smile, and I thought he was kinda cute.

He went on. "Anyway, appreciate your looking out for him. Just take him down to Security. They'll take it from there. You'll have to go up to the second floor. When you get off the elevator, turn right, then look for the first hallway on the right, about ten doors down, middle of the corridor."

As he was pointing, I looked to see if he was wearing a wedding band on his left hand. I always automatically sort of do that, you know what I mean? He wasn't.

"The Security office is the second door on the left. Got that? Second floor, right off the elevator, right at the first hallway, second door on the left. Ok?"

I thanked the officer and took George's hand. We walked toward the elevator. When we got off on the second floor, we turned left and went straight out to my car.

I rummaged through the cupboards in my apartment, looking for some food George could eat. I found some peanut butter, crackers, and half of a banana left over from my breakfast. He ate quickly and seemed to like it. But, there was still no smile, and he wasn't saying anything.

While he ate, I drew warm water into the tub and added some bubble bath, then threw a few plastic containers from the kitchen into the tub for him to play with. I fetched a towel and washcloth and one of my shirts that he could wear as a nightshirt.

With George playing in the tub, I stayed in the room, picked up his dirty clothes, and filled the washbasin with soap and water. I checked the pockets of his shorts and pulled out a soft, half-eaten Godiva chocolate bar. From Hilley's, probably. When George saw the candy bar, he reached his hand toward it and pleaded with his eyes. Still no words.

"It's ok, George. I'll set it here. You can have it after your bath. Don't worry."

His arm stayed in the air a bit longer. But, when I didn't give it to him, he went back to playing. Before I dressed him in the nightshirt, I gave him a bite of the chocolate.

I wanted to read him a bedtime story, but of course, I had no children's books. I did have the Sunday newspaper, though, and decided the comics would have to do. George didn't resist when I pulled him onto my lap. I think he was starting to trust me. The pictures in the comics were good. Since he wouldn't understand the jokes, I made up some words to go with the "Garfield", "Peanuts", and "Hagar the Horrible" strips.

Then I tucked him into my bed. He fell asleep while I was singing "My Favorite Things" from Sound of Music. I love that song. I kissed his forehead and grabbed my other pillow before turning out the lights. I felt this – whatta you call it? – like a sense of contentment. I tucked sheets into my sofa and slept there, one ear listening for George that night.

———

When I heard the knock on the door, I do have to say, my whole body lurched. It wasn't that I wasn't expecting it. I just didn't want this time with George to come to an end. It felt so right to me. George and me.

George was sitting on the living room floor, creating towers and roads with some shoeboxes and pushing empty toilet roll tubes down ramps and off imagined cliffs. He was absorbed and didn't look up when I opened the door. But, he became interested when two police officers and Grant, the security guy from the mall, came in.

When they saw the boy and me, they looked at the picture they were holding. Grant nodded to the police officers. One of the officers grabbed my arms and snapped handcuffs on me. The other spoke. "Sally Steward? We have a warrant for your arrest for the kidnapping of Brian …" At first, I was confused. I didn't know any Brian. Then I got it.

He read me my rights. Then a woman stepped up to the doorway. She went over to George and told him everything would be ok, and she was taking him to a safe place. He would have other children to play with there. Grant stood by with a very sick look on his face. I thought he might throw up or something.

The woman pulled George to his feet. He stood still, just watching, listening. He stared at me with the biggest frown. Then, in the sweetest voice I have ever heard, "Mum-Mum," he said. "Mum-Mum."

I guess I was numb when the judge gave me five years in prison. My attorney said I could get out in three for good behavior.

That's what I did. I survived it. I minded my own business, did what I was told to do. I was relieved when I got kitchen duty instead of toilets. It could have been worse.

An old guard watched me in the kitchen, wiping down those big counters, straightening up the dish towels on the racks, sweeping up. His belly always pushed out against his shirt, and there was a button missing down there close to his belt. One day, I told him I could sew a button on for him if he wanted. He just smirked. But a few days later, I was reassigned to the laundry room. He and some of the other guards started bringing their uniforms and personal clothes in for me to repair. It worked out. I got the "three years, good behavior" deal.

When I got out, they gave me the clothes I was wearing when I was arrested, and a little money for the bus and some food. On automatic pilot, I took the bus from town to my old neighborhood. My landlord had moved my stuff to the basement and rented out my apartment. I had nowhere to go. When I saw the mall, I got off. I could hang out there and figure out what to do next.

I went to the food court and found a table in the corner. I watched people come and go. When someone left food or coffee on the table, I snatched it. My mind was like frozen. I had no idea of where to go or what to do next.

I could hear the clatter of vendors closing up. I stared at the table, twiddling a straw between my fingers, not really thinking of anything. But then I heard a voice behind me. He told me the mall was closed. I wanted to crawl under the table.

He came around, and I saw his head jerk back when he saw my face. I think I must've jerked too. It was Grant. Grant Peasely. That sad-looking Security Guard. He was a little bit grayer, but, yeah, that was definitely him. The tone of his voice changed when he saw my face.

"Um... so you got out then? Sally, isn't it?"

I nodded. "Today."

"Good. Good. Ok, then." He paused. "I'm sorry, but the mall's closing and you have to go. Um ..."

I picked up the paper cup and plate and walked to the trash can. He watched me.

"Here, I'll go with you and unlock the door to let you out." He must have remembered how he had failed to escort George and me to the Security office.

We walked down the long corridor in silence. As we neared the exit door, he asked, "Do you have somewhere to go? I mean, home, family?"

I shook my head. He opened the door, and we stepped into the entryway. But instead of opening the outer door, he pointed to a bench against the wall. "Do you mind sitting here for a minute? I mean, just for a minute, and I'll come back, ok?"

He went back inside, and I saw him bend over to retie his shoes. While bent over, he glanced once or twice up at the ceiling. Then he returned. He coughed. "Listen. I can't send you out there in this weather. I mean, I'd like to help you ... you know?"

"I need you to wait here another hour, ok? Like you're waiting for a bus. Um ... I have to lock the door into the mall, but the outer door will be unlocked." He lowered his voice and whispered, "In an hour, the shop owners will be gone. I'll be back for you then. One hour." His voice hurried. "I'll come by and wave as if I'm asking you to leave. When I do this, I want you to go out the door and turn to your right. Before you reach the end of the building, there's a white door. There's no handle on the outside. Go stand in front of that door and wait until I open it. One hour from now, ok?" I nodded, and he disappeared.

———

The snowflakes landing on my nose and cheeks revived something in me, a sort of joyful feeling of being alive, being outdoors. It was then I realized I was free! Nowhere to go, but free!

The thought of being out of prison gave me such a rush that I found myself spreading my arms and turning 'round in circles. My face was turned toward the sky, and the cold drops of snow were running from my face, down my neck, and into the V-neck of my shirt, onto my breasts. It was glorious!

The white-door-without-a-handle opened, and Grant stood in the shadows. He didn't say anything at first. Just stood there watching me dance in the polka-dotted moonlight. But before too long, he whispered, "Sally, come in, hurry!"

He led me down a dark, narrow hallway. I couldn't see. I groped the rough walls and took tiny steps. I felt his hand press on my arm, then slide down to take my hand in his to pull me along. The hallway opened up to a large room with dim lights, crowded with furniture. Grant continued to hold my hand as he dodged sofas, tables, and recliners. We reached the next room, also crowded, but this time with beds. There were shelves along the walls with comforters. He dropped my hand and bent over a large bin. Then he shoved a pillow into my arms. A few steps later, he grabbed a blanket from a table marked, *CLEARANCE*.

We went to the back corner of the room. There was a bed made up with a floral comforter and pillows in shams. Grant pointed to a red neon *EXIT* sign. "Restrooms," he said. He reached into his pocket and pulled out a small flashlight, and he handed it to me. What he did next was a surprise. He pulled a side of the comforter up onto the bed. It wasn't a mattress at all underneath the bed coverings. It was a bed-sized plywood frame built to resemble a bed so the store could display bedding. Huh! Who would have known? He lifted the lid and motioned for me to climb inside. "You can sleep here. You'll have to leave at four. I'll come back for you."

Really? Get into this box? But, I didn't waste any time. I threw the blanket and pillow in and climbed inside. The lid closed.

Now I knew what the flashlight was for. I turned it on right away because being in a box was giving me the creeps. Better, with a little light.

I surveyed my new digs. The light caught something sparkling to my left. I shone the light on it, picked it up, and saw it was a gold candy wrapper.

I pulled half of the blanket over me and sunk my head into the new pillow. Lying still, I realized how tired I was. I thought it wasn't too bad. I should be able to fall asleep. But, unable to settle, I continued to move the light up and down the walls and in the corners, then stopped 'cause I noticed something else. Directly above me, I saw a small, brown handprint. I sat up and sniffed. Chocolate. I lay back down and kept the light shining on the handprint. Well, I'll be …

I felt a hand on my shoulder, shaking me out of my sleep. Grant whispered, "Time to go." He waited for me while I used the restroom. We went out into the darkness, the way we had come in. A Security SUV was waiting outside the door. He pointed, and I climbed into the front passenger seat. As soon as he got in, he started talking really fast. He said he had three more nights working night turn before his weekend. If I needed a place to sleep that night, I could go back to the same entrance at ten o'clock and wait for him. Same routine. If I didn't show up, it was ok. No problem. He'd come by to check.

I didn't know what to say, wondered why he was being so nice to me, then I remembered the handprint. That's just the kind of guy he is, I thought. Wanting to help people.

He dropped me off at the end of the parking lot and pulled away without a goodbye. I stood there for a minute, raised my hand to my shoulder, thought of his hand touching me there earlier.

The next three nights, Grant put me to bed and woke me in the morning. I started to think I could get used to that. On that last morning, when he was driving me to the end of the lot to drop me off, he said one thing. He said I could sleep on the sofa in his apartment – not for long – but until I got my own place. I just nodded. When I opened the door to get out, he said, "Same routine, same entrance at closing, I'll pick you up." And that was that.

Turns out, Grant and I were pretty good roommates. He gave me space, and I kept it neat. He bought food, and I cooked. We took turns doing dishes.

I spent my days looking for a job. Ha! I ended up with two jobs. There was a dry cleaners in a strip of shops across from the mall. I spoke with the manager. I was honest and told him where I had gotten laundry experience. I used my probation officer and Grant as references. I went back a week later and was hired.

The hair salon at the mall also hired me to sweep and clean. I had been going there for haircuts for years. Then one day – it was a busy day – I was asked to give a shampoo. There was a long wait for the stylist, so I gave the customer a good scalp massage. She raved so much to the stylist that they gave me more customers. You wouldn't believe the tips women give for a nice scalp massage.

While I was at Grant's place, we started flirting a bit. We got, well, I'd call it affectionate. Not too much, like teasing and bumping shoulders, not moving our hands away when they accidentally touched, eye-talk, that kinda stuff. We laughed a lot, too. Now, we're starting to be more than roommates, if you get my drift.

So, that's about it – the story of how Grant and I met. I guess you could say that if it weren't for George, it never would have happened. Funny how life works that way. It turned out that meeting George was what helped me to find Grant. Still, there was somethin' … somethin' right about George and me. Sweet little thing. Makes me smile when I think of him. Wonder how he's gettin' on.

Oh, there is one last thing I want to tell you. One Sunday, during my break at the hair salon, I was sitting on a bench in the mall drinking a Slurpee or something. I saw three boys walking the corridor in my direction. They were joking around, awkward, bumping into each other. About eight, nine years old, I'd guess. When they got to about, um, two stores away, the boy in the middle stopped cold. The other two kept going. The boy who stopped was tall and skinny, and his shirt was too short, showing a little skin. Not sure if that was on purpose or not. His blond hair almost covered his eyes, but I could tell he was staring at me. Serious face. I smiled at him. Then – and I'm not making this up – I could swear that his lips moved, and he said, "Mum-Mum." After that, he took off and ran past me to catch up with his buddies.

The Vixen's Tail

The white van hovered in her rearview mirror, and it stuck to her back bumper like an insect on flypaper when she made the abrupt, sharp left turn. Julie's eyes darted between the van behind her and the eerie sight of an empty, grass-littered parking lot in front of her. The car swerved. Julie's mind went into overdrive. A flush crept up her neck, sat on her cheeks, and simmered there.

"Apocalypse," she thought. Dread and uncertainty stirred within her inner bank of "feelings to be squashed and avoided." She struck the steering wheel with both palms and whispered, "Damn this pandemic!"

There was no one in the lot ahead, but Julie came to a complete stop at the stop sign. "Rules are rules" was a maxim she lived by. A long blast from the horn behind her insisted she change her way of thinking. Every nerve in her body jumped. The long curls of her black-streaked red hair tumbled over her face and the steering wheel as she hunched forward.

The shadow of a van pulled up next to her. She inched closer to the steering wheel. The rumble of deep bass rhythms coming from behind closed windows reached through her windows and shook her world. She could feel his eyes on her, and she tried to look at him through a gap in her hair. She saw only an orange construction vest. The screech of tires as he peeled off gave her yet another start.

"Idiot!" Her mother shouted from the back seat.

She heard a sharp, yet distant and muted clash of metal when her mother released her seat belt. It had been a surreal drive on the deserted highway, and now, the man's harassment was pushing her up against a familiar tipping point. She knew what would come next. Her own mind was about to lead the attack against her. The tension was sweeping her head clear of any sense of stability. Her stomach felt as if it had collapsed, trying to escape from her body. Sweat was forming on her forehead and at the back of her neck.

Unable to concentrate while trying to move the car to the curb, her foot jumped between gas pedal and brake, and the car moved in fits and starts. She opened her door and put her feet on the ground, but the car still felt as if it were moving. "Darn!" She returned her foot to the brake pedal and shifted into *PARK*.

Both feet on the ground again, she bent forward to place her head in her hands. Her mother's hand on her shoulder startled her. The hand moved slowly down her back and began to trace circles meant to soothe. A chant drifted through the fog, "Shhh, it's ok. Shhh, you're ok. He's gone now. We're good now. Shhh, you're ok, we're ok."

Julie began to count her breaths, an accustomed habit now. "In, 2, 3, 4, 5, 6, 7, 8. Hold, 2, 3, 4. Out, 2, 3, 4, 5, 6, 7, 8. In …" After seven cycles, nausea would begin to subside. The weakness of having fought a battle would remain for hours.

With a deep inhale, she remembered why she was there and forced herself to sit up. "I'm ok, Mom. Go. You're going to be late." Crossing her arms in a tight hug, she rocked forward, back.

"Are you sure, Julie? I can call and …"

"No, get in there. Your tooth. They're waiting for you."

There was a squeeze on her shoulder and the sound of the rear door opening and closing. As her mother crossed in front of the car, a limp wave and a blown kiss were all she could muster.

Julie scanned the parking lot. The white van was nowhere to be seen. "You're ok. Breathe. You can't just sit here. You have to park in a space."

She saw a line of trees in the first row, opposite the end corner of the shopping center. The shade would help. After running her front tires up against a cement curb in a shaded spot, she opened her window for air.

"Find your phone, Julie. Just in case."

She pulled her cell phone from her bag and held it in her lap, then stared out at the empty lot. Paintings on the building at the other end of the lot swirled in front of her. Skeletons dancing on the stucco walls brought another wave of nausea. She rested her head on the steering wheel.

"In, 2, 3, 4 ..."

The sound of a car roused her, and her back stiffened. The driver parked nearby, then got out and went into the dentist's office. In sitting up, she had glimpsed something out of the corner of her eye. "What was that? A flicker of orange?" But when she turned to look, there was nothing. "I'm so jumpy."

The heat in the car was stifling. She got out and leaned against the car door, and focused her sight on the peaceful woods behind the shopping center.

"In, 7, 8. Hold, 2, 3 ..." Her mind traveled back in time, back to when the panic attacks began....

She's in seventh grade. She's sitting in the last row in the classroom, where she has been told to sit, so her bushy hair won't block anyone's view. She's being teased about how she looks, and she believes what they are saying. Scene change. Now, she's in the empty school parking lot that she crosses after each piano lesson. In the fading evening light, a boy comes up from behind....

His name, she refused to remember. His sneer, she would never forget.

There was movement in the woods. A sparkle. "A flash of orange again?"

She snapped to attention as an animal emerged from the thick brush and made a dash for the trash cans on the side of the building. The volume of her heartbeat went up.

"A dog? No, it wasn't a dog. Was it a raccoon?"

Reaching the fenced-in barrels, just three car lengths from where she stood, the animal came to a sudden halt. Its head lifted and turned toward Julie, and it glared at her with its yellow eyes. Julie gazed at the animal with her pale yellow-green eyes, and she was struck with recognition and awe.

"It's a red fox! I've never heard of a red fox being seen in these crowded suburbs!"

Julie remained still, studying. Water droplets from the marshy grasses glistened on the dense red hair. The pointed ears, tipped in black, seemed to be acutely listening. With its tail swinging wildly back and forth, she could see that the fox sensed danger.

Moments passed. Julie's fear gave way to humility in the face of the creature's beauty. A calm feeling of familiarity wrapped around her. Images from her childhood called on her sympathies. Watching the fox triggered a memory....

Her father is giving a new stuffed fox to their puppy Max. She falls instantly in love with it. Her father leaves the room, and she throws a ball for Max to chase. With Max distracted, she grabs the furry toy and tucks it under her shirt. The fox sleeps hidden in her bed that night and every night thereafter....

———

As Julie's heartbeat slowed down, the tail of the red fox became calm. It extended out horizontally with the tip lifted upward, waving ever so slightly. Its effect on Julie was like that of a magic wand.

She became entranced. She thought, "It's friendly. It wants to come close."

She had to restrain her curiosity and desire to reach out and touch the animal's bristly head. Instead, she conveyed her respect and affection in mind only and continued to remain still. Her breath, the breeze, the sunlight, the seconds – all seemed to be moving in slow motion.

"Tick ... tick ... tick ..." The fox sat back on its bushy tail, exposing patches of white on its belly. "tick ... tick ..." Julie opened her hands in front of her, tilted her head to the side, and sent a closed-lipped smile to the fox. "tick ... tick ... tick ..." The fox bent its front legs and extended black-booted paws along the ground toward Julie. "tick ... tick ..." In return, Julie bowed her head toward the fox.

They remained in this pose for several seconds until the quiet was interrupted by a booming bass sound and the squeal of wheels turning into the parking lot from the road. A white van with ladders on the roof and no signs on the side passed between them. Julie's eyes followed as it sped by her. When she looked back, the fox was gone.

With air conditioning turned on low and doors locked, she settled into the bucket seat, her eyes and ears tuned to full alert mode. She saw the white van had parked in an empty lot next to a school building, at the far end of the lot in which she had parked.

The van door opened. She strained to get a look at the driver.

"Orange construction vest.   Good-looking, maybe. Twenties, early thirties?"

Even from this distance, with her 20/20 vision, she could see that he wore a fierce-looking scowl. He didn't look in her direction. He crossed the road and, as he turned the corner by the dancing skeletons, a buckle on his vest flashed a beam of sunlight, piercing her between the eyes. She was rubbing her forehead when he returned to the van, carrying a white Styrofoam container.

She kept one eye on the van while scrolling through Facebook pages on her phone, keeping her fidgety fingers busy. She wasn't paying attention to the screen.

"Did he recognize my car? Is he watching me?"

She was watching him. Cigarette smoke drifted out of the van window. She tried to send impatient orders to him using telepathy.

"Finish your lunch and leave already!"

It didn't work. Julie checked her phone to see if her mother had texted. She hadn't. Then she made sure she knew how to find the one-touch Emergency call button.

It was quiet. Julie wondered about the fox and how it had been able to survive in the suburbs. "Did it live on rodents and people's trash?" She had heard that wild animals were moving into the suburbs and cities with people staying inside during the pandemic.

Her thoughts returned to her puppy, Max, and to her father. "He must have caught on to my theft of the stuffed toy fox. He was probably amused. I hope he didn't think I was being mean. After this, he started reading *The Fox and the Crow* from *Aesop's Fables* to me at bedtime. He always embellished the story with his own observations." She could hear her father's gentle voice....

———

"One day, a fox went out for a walk in the forest. She brushed against a tree's bark to comb her bushy red hair and black-streaked tail. Just like your hair, Julie. Beautiful hair!

"The fox heard a rustle in the leaves above her. She turned her shiny, yellow eyes – like yours, Julie – up toward the sound. She crinkled her long, straight nose at what she saw. You do that too, sometimes, don't you, Sweetie?"

He smiles and pulls her closer with a hug.

"The fox saw a crow with a morsel of cheese at the tip of his beak. The fox was hungry and wanted the cheese for herself. She couldn't reach the crow and had to come up with a plan to get the cheese. Foxes are very intelligent and clever, you know. Like you, Julie. You're smart and clever too.

"The fox knew what she had to do. She spoke to the crow. 'Hello, Crow! You have the most beautiful feathers I've ever seen, so black and sleek. I think you must also have a fine voice to match. Tell me, is your voice as grand as your handsome coat?'

"The crow was flattered and pleased. It was rare to receive such compliments. He opened his mouth to impress the fox with his voice. Do you know what happened next, Julie?"

Julie turns to face her father. "I do, Papa. The piece of cheese fell from the crow's mouth to the ground. The fox picked up the cheese and ran off while the crow was still singing."

They laugh. Julie and her father and her little stuffed fox are quite impressed and content with this ending....

A blue pickup truck jolted her when it came up from behind and continued past her. When it parked next to the white van, she sat forward and craned to see. She began to shiver and turned off the air conditioning. The orange vest got out of the van, holding the Styrofoam container, and he leaned into the cab of the truck.

"Drugs? I'll bet he's selling drugs. It's a drug-free zone, idiot!"

She flipped to the camera on her cellphone, leaned closer to the windshield, and took two photos. When the orange vest pulled away from the truck, with his right hand in his pocket and no white container, she snapped another.

Then she worried.

"What if he saw me taking pictures?"

Julie double-checked to make sure her doors were locked and slid down in her seat, trying to become invisible. She surveyed the lot but saw only the empty car of the man who had entered the dentist's office. There was no sign of the fox.

"Come on, Mom. What's taking so long?"

Sunlight was beating against the windshield. She felt lightheaded again, and shivers rippled down her arms and spine.

"What if he comes after me?"

She listened for her father's voice.

"A fox went out for a walk. A fox went out.... Use your head, Julie."

She held her breath.

"Hold, 2, 3. Be smart, Julie, like the fox. Like the fox."

Her mind was racing....

The van drives toward her. It turns to come down the row where she's parked. It pulls up behind her car and stops.

"Out. Out. Out, 2, 3. I'm blocked in! There's a tree in front of my hood! What can I do?"

Her brain shifts into high gear. "The fox. The fox." She takes a deep breath. He gets out of the van.

She rolls down her window and smiles, hoping to put him off guard. "Oh, thank God for sending a handsome knight in shining armor to my rescue!"

She sees confusion cross his shadowed face. She watches him take it all in – her hair, her eyes, and her two longer-than-normal incisors that had been the cause of so much teasing. She hopes he won't see her legs trembling and wishes she hadn't worn such a short skirt.

"Could you give me a jump? I mean, ah ... my car won't start, and my cell phone just died. I have cables in the trunk. But you'll have to pull around to the front for the cables to reach. Here, wait a minute."

She leans toward the passenger seat to reach for her phone, stretching her long slender calf out through the open door horizontally. She flexes her foot upward and waves it ever so slightly, like a friendly vixen's tail.

She sits up and holds her powered-down phone out the window. "Nope, still not working. I appreciate that you're such a gentleman. I'll bet you're as good on the inside as you are on the outside."

His head tilts, and his brow furrows while pondering this. He seems to be dazzled. His eyes are glazed, and his jaw is slack. The magic has worked – he is spellbound. As he turns to return to his van, Julie's nose twitches.

The van moves forward to come around to face her. She waits until it reaches the end of the row, and then she backs her car out with a squeal and spins the car in the opposite direction. As she rushes off, she waves to him through her open window. Her lips curl, and her chest expands with the air she has been struggling to find.

She feels victorious. And clever....

The door to the dentist's office opened and nudged Julie out of her reverie. She looked across the lot and saw the white van still sitting next to the school. She held her breath when the van started to back out of the parking spot. Her fingernails dug into her palm. The van turned right, moving away from her, and charged toward the closest exit, where it sped through the red light. Her held breath escaped as short barking "out" sounds blown through her puckered lips. She started the car and chided herself for the tricks that her runaway mind could play.

Julie's mother climbed into the back seat and leaned forward. "How are you feeling now, dear? I was so worried."

Julie tugged against her seat belt, attempting to turn. "I'm good now, Mom. Really. I'm over it. How about you? Was the dentist able to do something?"

The answer was lost to her as her focus went to the yellow eyes in her rearview mirror. A flicker of orange faded into the woods as she gave a parting nod.

Sicilian Postcards

Anno 2004, Palermo, Sicily

Ciao Famiglia e Amici,

Today, I am a guest in Palermo, Sicily,
rapt with the marvel of a passing parade.
Squinting, gowned patients sneeze in the daylight,
bouncing in wheelchairs, railed beds pushed by aides.
The steady stream moves from old hospital to new.
Carriages are wheeled, then lifted and tipped
over curbs, concrete sidewalks, along winding way
toward a palace-resplendent, seeming fairytale-made.
Golden doors open magically to reveal marble walls
and floors with shine to rival a Mediterranean sun's glow.
New residents pray with folded hands, voices low,
"Dear God, have I died and gone to Paradiso?"

A fitting celebration for the hospital's opening day!
I watched from beneath an orange tree,
imagined the scents — woody, astringent,
fresh-cut spruce masking disinfectant detergent,
walls not yet soaked with illness and death.

I fell in love with the pageantry,
the pragmatism of Palermo!
"Dear God, have I died and gone to Paradiso?"

Must sleep now. More later.
Arrivederci! Amore!

Anno 1144, Monte Pellegrino, Palermo, Sicily

Fourteen-year-old Rosalia
grabs hold of rock, tree, and brush
as she climbs Monte Pellegrino.
Daylight is fading, and she is alone.
Focused intent creases her brow.
Resolve makes taut her plum, slender lips.
She flees from a Prince to whom she has been promised.
She will live her own life, not that of a wife.
Climbing toward solitude, she reaches for God.

The townspeople search for their dear Rosalia,
descendant of Charlemagne,
born of noble rose merchant,
beloved daughter of Palermo.
Prince, family, servants, clergy,
and faithful search and pray.
As they had rejoiced on the day of her birth,
waved with giddiness as she rode through the town,
gave thanks for her presence in the grand Cattedrale,
the townspeople now wept in mourning for
their lovely, adored, blessed child, Rosalia.

Anno 2004, Palermo, Sicily

Buona Sera, Cara Familigia!

My window is open for the warm breeze and
I am listening to faint music and voices

floating in from a marionette performance.

The hand-carved wooden puppets,
dressed in bright paints and striking detail
are made here in Sicily.
The music is weaving in and out with
the background sound of
revving engines and honking Fiats, and with
the alternating bass and soprano sirens
of la polizia and ambulanza.
These are the sounds of Palermo at night.

This morning, I dove into the island's swift flow.
I walked to work, crossing eight busy streets.
As I dodged motorbikes and Smart cars,
I couldn't escape the feeling of being
a character in a video game.
Vehicles must, by law, stop for pedestrians, but …
one must learn to trust!
I step off the curb, hold my breath,
and believe in miracles.

Come, dear ones, walk along with me
through the labyrinthine maze of this seaside city!

Let's bypass leaning scaffolds
fronting ancient, crumbling walls
and take care not to trip
over scattered sleeping dogs.
The dogs run free but, as you can see,
they have a preference for lounging.
Here are fruit stands, pizzerias,

espresso bars lined five rows deep.
La panetteria window is dressed
with fruit-shaped marzipan
in yellows, reds, and greens.

Church towers, though forbidding, beckon,
while la Cattedrale glimmers in glory.
Now, look at the government guards over there.
Carabinieri carry long rifles — carabina.
Let's tiptoe, and remember, don't stare!

Children are skipping on their walk to school –
girls hold hands and play clapping games;
boys bump and joke, stealing glances at the girls.
An abandoned doll watches
from a sun-swept lonely stoop.

At the corner, in a small park,
are several gray-haired men,
though it is only 7 a.m.
Some are playing card games.
Shoulders touching, others speak.
Before moving on, they kiss on both cheeks.

After work, I say, we're in for a treat –
we'll go for la cena!
Frutti di Mare, Fava Bean Frittata,
Pasta with Sardines, Swordfish Caponata,
Vino Nero D'Avola, and Gelato Nocciola.

Next weekend, we'll visit Market Vucciria
and taste swordfish, octopus, eel, bluefin tuna.

We'll see the opera at Teatro Massimo.
Oh, how we'll cry at the finale tragico.
On Sunday, we'll step out for an after-dinner stroll.
It is Palermitani tradition for the locals of Palermo.

Grazie for joining me. I miss you all!
Amore!

Anno 1631, Palermo, Sicily

The bubonic plague has ravaged Italy
for two years. A million have died.
In Palermo, a man, following vision or escape,
climbs Monte Pellegrino.
Wandering, fatigued, he blesses himself
when he sees a cave and enters for rest and shelter.
The dripping of chilled water from the ceiling
smooths patches of the sharp-edged walls and
forms rivulets that run along furrows in the rough floor.
The cave reaches deep into darkness.
He lights his torch and scans
for dry and protective cover from the wild.
In the glow of his flame, a spot of white
at the foot of the dark walls startles.
With what animals does he share this space?
With caution, he moves closer, then kneels
when he finds the bones of a woman.

He remembers the legend of Rosalia,
imagines her story, her fate. Wonders.

Was it starvation? Poison berries? Old age?
What was the destiny
for one in need of solitude and prayer,
for one with dreams of living on her own terms?

Anno 2004, 2 Nov., La Festa Dei Morti, Palermo, Sicily

Awake, Bambini!
Look at the sweets and toys Nonna has left you!
You have been good to pray for her soul!

Piacere! Hi! Hello!

This morning I awoke to a howling wind.
The dead had come for their annual visit.
On my walk to work, I held onto fences and walls
and feared I would be blown away.
A metal panel, loose on three corners, clattered and
slammed against an iron rail fence in my passageway.
Hurry! Spedire!

By noon, the wind had become calm and the sun warm.
Sparkles leapt from the puddles – invitations from the dead
to meet at the cemetery for a family picnic.
The bambini chanted, "Pupi a cena! Pupi a cena!"
for the knight and lady sugar dolls.

Remembering our loved ones,

Baci e Abbracci … Kisses and Hugs

Anno 1631, Palermo, Sicily

"Rosalia has been found!"
shout the townspeople of Palermo.
"Rosalia, our beloved!
Bring her bones to la Cattedrale.
There she can get some rest.
Bring her home."

The five-hundred-year-old bones
are placed into a jewel-laden box,
fit for a princess.
By horseback, the rescuers journey down
a winding, narrow trail and across
three miles of dirt roads to the city of Palermo,
weaving up and down streets
before their final stop.
The residents gather to witness the arrival of
fourteen-year-old Rosalia.

> *Let it be known that*
> *on the very day*
> *that Rosalia's bones*
> *were paraded through Palermo*
> *and were laid to rest in la Cattedrale,*
> *the bubonic plague in Italy*
> *came to an end!*

"A miracle! A Saint!!" the residents declared.
"Rosalia has driven the plague away and
healed the citizens of Italy!"

In a hotel by the sea,
a Flemish artist in quarantine
salutes the occasion with a portrait of Rosalia.
Upon her head, he places a wreath of roses.
Cherubs, skull, and prayer book float about her.

Anno 1901, Pittsburgh Pennsylvania, U.S.A.

Sons of Italy cross the Atlantic
to answer the call of a revolution.
Industry is thriving in America.
In the smoky city of Pittsburgh,
iron, steel, glass, brick, and rail
are produced, and work is abundant.
Families follow, and eyes turn
to the building of church and school.

A church of red brick and simple adornment
is graced with Rosalia's name.
To the left of the altar, her statue stands
gazing out across the nave,
with a wreath of roses upon her head,
skull and prayer book in her hands.

Anno 2005, Monte Pellegrino, Palermo, Sicily

Miei Cari … My Dear Ones,

Today, I climbed the shadowed Monte Pellegrino,

bouncing in the back seat of a Fiat taxi.

We stopped at an overlook to see
Palermo in the distance below.
Roses and lilies covering the mountainside
waved in the breeze.

I thought of the church in Pennsylvania,
bearing the name of Palermo's Rosalia.
In the parade of babies baptized,
the year the church was built,
was one christened Helen Rosalia,
who would one day become my nonnina.

In the atrium of a cave, the legend of Rosalia lives on.
Plaster casts, crutches, and dented cycle fenders
are nailed to a wall. There, flapping in the wind
are cards of gratitude from the cured and the saved,
and prayerful requests for mending;
prayers to the Patroness of Healing,
to the Patroness of Palermo,
to the Patroness of my family for three generations;
prayers to Rosalia, who, with a divine connection,
had lifted the plague from Italy.

Inside il Santuario, cave water from the dripping ceiling
is channeled into a vat for visitors.
In this space, which Rosalia called home,
the air feels holy. Blessed.
I could sense her healing presence.

As I returned down Monte Pellegrino to Palermo

a love song played softly through the radio speakers.

The driver watched me in his rearview mirror
and must have caught the tear that slipped
as I thought of Rosalia's resilience and determination
and remembered prayers answered through the years.

Blessed.

Arrivederci, Sicilia, sempre nel mio cuore,
always in my heart!
See you soon, dear ones! Coming home.

Every Anno, 15 July, Palermo, Sicily

A solemn procession winds through the streets of Palermo.
A jeweled box rides high upon a carriage.
Reverent crowds, with faces raised, are chanting,
"Rosalia! Rosalia! Rosalia!"

References and Notes – Sicilian Postcards

(1) Alfani, Guido; Percoco, Marco (2019). "Plague and long-term development: the lasting effects of the 1629–30 epidemic on the Italian cities" (PDF). *The Economic History Review*
Note: During the bubonic plague of 1629-1631, "it can be estimated that overall 30- 35 per cent of the northern Italian population died, amounting to about two million victims."

(2) https://www.worldometers.info/coronavirus/
Note: Anno 2021, August
Sicilian Postcards was written during the 2020-2021 Covid-19 pandemic. In the first eighteen months, the virus infected worldwide over 215 million people and caused 4.4 million deaths, with close to 129,000 deaths in Italy (0.21% of the population) and more than 649,000 deaths in the United States (0.19% of the population).

(3) Sucato, Ignazio, *Santa Rosalia – Patrona Di Palermo – II Edizione*, Edizioni LA VIA Palermo, 1978, IMPRIMATUR Curia Arcivescovile di Palermo-14 Gennaio 1976 + Angelo Cella, Vescovo Ausiliare

(4) Jason Farago, "The Saint Who Stopped An Epidemic", *New York Times*, March 27, 2020, Section C, p. 1
Note: Anthony van Dyck, a Flemish artist, was quarantined in Palermo during the plague and captured the moment with five paintings of Rosalia.

(5) "Diocese Saw Massive Growth In Early 20th Century", The
Pittsburgh Catholic Online,
https://www.pittsburghcatholic.org/news/diocese-saw-massive-
growth-in-early-20th-centurydiocese-of-pittsburgh-saw-massive-
growth-in-earl-20th-century-66131998

(6) St. Rosalia Church website,
https://ghocatholics.org/st-rosalia-site
Note: The website includes the history and a tour of St. Rosalia
Church

(7) G.M. Hopkins Company Maps for the City of Pittsburgh,
*Historic Pittsburgh Website, Hosted by the University of
Pittsburgh Library System,*

Title: Greenfield, Hazelwood, Plate 24. 1898.
https://historicpittsburgh.org/islandora/object/pitt%3A20090529-
hopkins-0026/viewer
Note: No church is shown and the property where St. Rosalia
Church was built is privately owned.

Title: Greenfield. Plate 22. 1904. .
https://historicpittsburgh.org/islandora/search/catch_all_fields_mt
%3A%2804v01p22%29
Note: St. Rosalia Church is shown in its original location.

Title: Greenfield. Plate 23A. 1923.
https://historicpittsburgh.org/islandora/object/pitt%3A23v0223a/vi
ewer
Note: St. Rosalia Church, Grade School, and High School are
shown.

(8) Kulina, Anita, *Millhunks and Renegades, A Portrait of a Pittsburgh Neighborhood*, Brandt Street Press, 2003. pp. 77-78, 91

(9) Marjorie Coll, "Ad Multos Annos", *St. Rosalia Review*, Volume 1, Number 2, May 1938
Note: The article specifies that St. Rosalia School was built twenty-five years earlier or in 1913.

David Baker

An Era Lost

Upon the Face of This Earth

Searching

Coming Late

Tradition

The Story of Granddad Hibbitt

Ice Cream

Is Mankind Born Evil?

Walter

I came to America from a country in which Shakespeare, Dickens, Keats, and Wordsworth, and so many others, dominated literature. They were all wordsmiths.

I attended a school that was founded in 1557. How about that for tradition? We boys were divided into four houses named after: the poet Blackmore; the playwright Garrick; a satirical poet Pope; and the writer Walpole. All wordsmiths, no scientists, no explorers, not even a politician.

I was in the house of Pope and studied under the guidance of traditional, classically trained teachers, who talked, and talked, and talked. Could we ever stop them? So, I grew up in a culture in which words were everything. What chance did I have of escaping all those words?

Because of that background, I have never felt like Eliza Doolittle in My Fair Lady, who gave us:

"Words, words, words.
I'm so sick of words
I get words all day through
First from him, now from you.
Is that all you blighters can do?"

. . . but I have long understood the sentiment.

Today, we require instant messages to be relayed immediately rather than after we have taken the time to consider and ponder. With a pen in hand or even the typewriter keyboard in front of us, there were opportunities to consider. But now, it seems we no longer want to think about and design what we want to communicate. Everything is instant.

However, I insist on remaining traditional, wordy, and the devout product of my background. I like the words and what they can convey. Our language is so rich, each word with a variety of meanings. I like the challenge of choosing *le mot juste*—the exact word. There, you see, even the French agree with the idea!

Messages need to be crafted. I believe writing is an art form. That's why I write.

During my various careers I started to write a book about my growing up in England. It is a series of vignettes about traditional life being overturned by the events in the first half of the last century, growing up in the war under the threat of being bombed, living with a strict father, and having to abide by the limits of outdated conventions. I plan to have this published next year.

Meanwhile, I have dabbled in poetry, a children's story, and expressions of other thoughts and ideas that have flitted through my mind. I hope you will enjoy the results of my efforts, especially all the words.

An Era Lost

Unlike Dylan Thomas's town, there wasn't always snow in our village. When it did come, its settling was cause for rejoicing and merriment. But once the cold has taken its grip, the wind and rain of an English winter permit no dawdling on the necessary shopping trips. Villagers, bundled up in hats, heavy coats, and woolen scarves, scurry from shop to shop, reluctant to share even the shortest exchange with others for fear the chill will penetrate the layers of clothing they have pulled together for the outing.

The bright lights and colorful Christmas displays can be passed by for now and perused later once a break in the weather allows a stroll. Light spills out on the pavement and street, pushing back the winter darkness and spreading a warm welcome to all. The old buildings seem to take on a renewed glow as if preening themselves for the seasonal attention they receive from both residents and visitors.

There are two churches in our village. Saint John's on High Street, now rather sad and almost neglected, was one of the first buildings to be built in our village hundreds of years ago. Now people visit rarely. Lack of attention has paid a toll. The congregation, numbered in single digits, consists of the more elderly, widows garbed in black, with beliefs that religion is a very serious business.

By contrast, All Saints, a hundred years newer and built of a warmer stone, is very popular, especially at Christmas time. The organ music seems lighter and more embracing; the jovial minister accepting of all. The brightness, the warmth, and the welcome are more soothing to the soul than the dry, forbidding biblical words at St. John's.

When Nanny Hibbitt, Mum's mother, came to visit, as she usually did around Christmas, she insisted on attending the drab

Saint John's. It was much more in keeping with her "traditional" and somber views about churches and religion.

"That's a proper church," I once heard her say. "I don't like the music at All Saints. And all those lights! That's not proper for a church. And that Vicar! He was laughing and. . . and. . ..he's too jovial.   You can't do that in church." So, we all had to go to ("dreary," I called it) Saint John's if Nanny happened to stay over on a Sunday.

As children, we felt the festive anticipation. It wasn't just Father Christmas and the possibility of presents. There was talk. There was speculation and planning. There was a new bustle, and whispering, and tantalizing secrets. There was something to look forward to… something!

Despite the bitter cold, Frank and Sydney were whooshing and whizzing again and again down the short hill behind the bike shop on their shiny red two-boy toboggan. Barry and Gladys were struggling to hold each other upright on the ice. Their skates slipped and slithered on the frozen Glidden Pond. There would be bruises tomorrow.

When the weather relented a little, Mrs. Porter would be out in front of her shop on High Street. That's the "I'm not a baker, I'm a pâtissier" Mrs. Porter, complete with her floppy toque and starched apron, as white as the snow beneath her black pointed shoes. She was offering warm cinnamon buns for passers-by to try.

"Merry Christmas, John." John Brand, our village cricket captain and our local policeman, was in his smart black uniform with the so-shiny buttons. He always stood at the intersection by the war memorial, hoping for more traffic to require his directing skills. Instead, he enjoyed the snatches of conversation and Christmas cheer with shoppers passing by with their parcels. He stopped every car he recognized just to share a laugh and goodwill.

John was a village stalwart, a symbol of the peace and orderliness that the residents appreciated and valued so much. Several of the teenage boys of the village had grown up remembering and honoring the lessons and homilies they had received when called in front of Mr. Brand to answer for some transgression. He was counselor, advisor, disciplinarian, and nobody had ever questioned or doubted the wisdom and common sense that came from the "iron hand in the black leather glove." As a disciplinarian, he sometimes supplanted a parent but no one could imagine our village without John Brand's correctness.

"What do you have, Mr. Harvey?" Our ancient greengrocer, with his green apron long enough to cause a tripping hazard, was also out in front of his shop holding a tray of fruit. Behind him, laid out like precious tree ornaments and looking as if they had been individually polished, were the fruits and vegetables of the season.

"These are Cox's Orange Pippins. The most delicious apple you ever tasted and just right to include in the Christmas pudding mixture. Beautiful apples! Very tasty! You have to try them." He cut pieces with his sharp knife and offered them out.

Making the Christmas pudding had a ritual to it, every year the same. Anyone who took a turn stirring the fragrant mixture was allowed one extra Christmas wish. Of course, this was Mum's way of getting some extra help in the kitchen. As the flour and butter and dried fruit and, of course, the rich mincemeat went into the bowl, so too would the old three-penny joeys that Dad had sterilized again after their use the previous year.

They had not been legal tender for over eighty years, but Dad had saved them carefully just for the Christmas pudding. The tiny, thin slivers of silver were mixed into the pudding, and if you were lucky enough to get one with your portion of the rich, heavy, nap-inducing dessert, then you had another special Christmas wish.

"How many have you put in, Dad?" Wendy asked, remembering that last year one joey was not recovered until the day after Boxing Day and nobody asked how or where it had been.

"I only have seven left, so everybody, remember that." He laughed as he stirred them in. Sadly, the number of joeys seemed to decline each year, and we all understood the importance of seeing just how many went in, so we could be sure they were all recovered afterward.

As a small boy, I was lucky two years to find a joey in my pudding but neither the million pounds nor the red Ferrari ever appeared. Perhaps the joeys were so old, they had lost their magic.

As villagers revered their cricket, the traditions of Christmas, and all the other long-embedded features of the English culture, a blanket of fear was spreading throughout the land. Before I was old enough to comprehend what was happening, much of the culture into which I was born was beginning to disappear. The thousands of years of tranquility, tradition, and stability in rural England were about to be desecrated. Adolph Hitler was plotting to conquer and plunder my peaceful homeland.

Upon the Face of This Earth

For however long I have
Upon the face of this earth
I need you here beside me
And with everything I am
Upon the face of this earth
I live to bring you happiness.
With all your love and caring
Upon the face of this earth
I'll strive to be much better.
For all I have become
Upon the face of this earth
I had your hand to guide me.
With all my love and devotion
Upon the face of this earth
I surround your every moment.
With all my heart and body
Upon the face of this earth
I cherish you completely
And everything I have
Upon the face of this earth
I give you unreservedly
And with the spirit from within me
Above the face of this earth
I'll be your love forever.

Searching

"I know it was here. I remember seeing it, at least in my mind's eye. It can't have gone far."

"Are you sure? If it was there nobody could have taken it or moved it. Or perhaps you moved it and put it somewhere else."

"It was right here. I know it was. Where could it have gone?" I pointed vainly in the general direction, my certainty beginning to fade as its absence became more and more apparent.

"Well then! It should still be there. Let's look for it again. Show me, where exactly was it?"

"Here," and I jabbed my finger on the surface.

But the surface wasn't there. My finger touched nothing. There was just space. There was a blackness all around my finger, and my hand, my arm, all around me. It was a bit like being in the dark. There didn't seem to be any points of reference, nothing there that I could relate to, nothing I could say with certainty that it was near there, or behind, or in front of. There was just this empty space—and the blackness. Is that where it should have been? Or is that where I thought I had seen it? Perhaps I didn't. I don't know. I was becoming uncertain. I pointed again but there was nobody there.

There was a growing sense of vagueness. Were my eyes not working right? Why couldn't I see? Was this strange feeling entirely in my head or was it my eyes that were playing tricks on me? Perhaps I should go and search for it somewhere else with the belief that if it were not where it was supposed to be then it had to be where it was not supposed to be. That's simple logic, isn't it? There is no point in continuing to search where it is not. Isn't that a version of that statement that Einstein was said to have made about doing it again and again and expecting a different result? And that leads to madness? Perhaps I'm going mad?

No. I'm not. I'm determined. It has to be somewhere else. I'll go somewhere else and search for it—but where? Where must I go? Where should I search? Where is the somewhere else where it might be? How can I hope to find it when I have no idea where I should start searching? This seems hopeless. This is all weird, all wrong. There's something wrong, isn't there? Everything is somehow out-of-control. There's nothing in its place. There is no place. There is nothing.

I hope it's not upstairs. I don't want to go upstairs. Not those stairs. I've tried to go up those stairs before, several times, and I've never made it all the way up. Why is that? Why can't I reach the top of the stairs?

But I have to do this? It's something I have to do. I have to keep searching, keep trying. I must. So I start to go up. The blackness is all around me and there is nothing to hold on to as I climb. No handrail.

As I climb each step, the blackness gets deeper and more enveloping. I'm climbing into nothing, just the next step going up. Nothing around me. Nothing around the stairs. Nothing above, nothing below the stairs. Just nothing! But I have to go up.

Progress is slow. It's getting harder to climb. Each stair step is taller than the one below. Each step seems to be closer to me, restricting my space. The stairs are becoming steeper and steeper. I'm reaching up for the next step, with my hands. It's above my head, like climbing a vertical cliff face. I can't do this. This is impossible. I simply can't do it.

And what am I searching for anyway?

Coming Late

Better an hour early
Than a single minute late
Mother said it often
As something she did hate
Punctuality's a habit
Can be good or bad
Politeness is a habit
With practice can be had
Early troubles no-one
Lateness always does
Offends the other people
And sets a negative buzz
Lateness causes trouble
The speaker must repeat
Everything said earlier
That's not an easy feat.
For all of those who came on time
Repetition's boring
Frustrates their looking forward
Their anticipation soaring
I know procrastination
Is popular nowadays
Some people cannot help it
Their mind's in such a haze
When you arrive early
You sometimes have to wait.

But it means you can get ready
For whatever is your fate
Now patience is a virtue
So, try hard not to hate
When you came nice and early
And someone walks in late.

Tradition

The words of the past will forever last, like a graveyard covered in
     mold
Running by like a persistent song they care nothing for getting old.
The message you hear is loud and clear, it speaks with a voice
     controlled.

The themes from the past dictate traditions that we must obey
Words said then are just like old men, they persist in having their
     say.
What has gone before will return once more and control us in
     every way.

The things we do now, the past has said how, completed long ago.
The straightjacket then will even say when, our thoughts restricted
     in flow.
To stop what we've heard is really absurd, we cannot deny what
     we know.

I'm always aware that the past is there, dragging along behind me
It lists our *shoulds* and knows our *coulds,* sets a path we cannot
     flee
The future's non-existent but memories are persistent, they tell us
     how to be.

So, before we begin, tradition will win any contest for how we
     should act
It was so before so now it is law, no matter how we react.
The die is cast, let's honor the past, and accept what it says as fact.

The Story of Granddad Hibbitt

I was growing up during World War II. So, the realization that people come and go in and out of our lives was real to me at a young age. Now that I am older, I have come to accept that some never leave us. They walk with us forever, bringing a smile to our face, a memory that is comforting. That one person for me is my maternal grandfather.

As a child, I was fascinated with his large droopy mustache. It was much fuller, almost chubbier than the one he had worn in the brown and yellowed photos I had seen taken before even my mother was born. His mustache matched his long white hair which always seemed to be a bit untidy. I don't think he was too bothered about that sort of thing.

Granddad was slow in voice, gentle, and softly spoken. He was never hurried and within himself there was a calm. He always had time for me, and I believe that was one of the reasons I was always comfortable with him and felt cared for and liked, maybe loved.

Grandad Hibbitt had been an amateur carpenter and a true lover of all items crafted in wood. He told me "Good wood wants you to hold it in your hands and feel its smoothness," and that you should always rub and caress wooden items.

I can recall the many occasions I visited his study. He would lift me up on his knee as he sat in front of his roll-top desk. To me as a young boy, it was so incredibly large. He showed me items and talked about them as if they were something mysterious or magical. I was fascinated.

He always had a treasure-trove of interesting things, different pens for doing the hand lettering that he was so good at, little cups and containers in carved wood, bottles of colored ink, erasers in holders, and all the other paraphernalia for writing and drawing. In the desk were rulers, set squares, and protractors. There were also pencils with different hardness of lead. Granddad told me that was for drawing lines of different thickness.

As a boy who loved practical and technical things, I just had to understand how his fountain pen worked, at a time when such things were still in their infancy. I remember my first examination, under his guidance. He filled the pen with ink from a bottle by operating a little lever at the side.

"Let's look inside," he said, as he unscrewed the two halves. Then he squeezed the inner sack. "What's this? Feel it. What's it made of?"

"It's rubber," I said as I pinched it. I remember the feel of the soft, silky rubber between my fingers.

"A little rubber tube. What happens to the air inside when I squeeze it?"

"It comes out," I remember saying, intrigued.

"Good. So, when I squeeze it and dip the end into the ink and let go of the tube, what will happen?" and he did that as he spoke. I watched spellbound as the ink flowed up into the tube between his fingers.

"The ink goes in." I was triumphant and turned to look at his smile. His long, white mustache wobbled as he laughed.

"Right. So now let's see how that can happen inside the pen." He lifted the little lever on the side of the barrel and showed me what happened inside. "That little piece there," and he pointed with a pencil, "presses and squeezes on the tube."

I thought the idea of a fountain pen was clever long before I knew anything about air pressure, which I later learned in a physics class.

Granddad put the pieces back together and operated the lever several times to show me the ink flowing out and then being sucked back in again. I looked up at him, and I believe probably conveyed to him my pleasure at being with him this way. It made me so proud that he took the time to be with me and think of me, even at the age of six.

I still treasure several small items he gave me and which he had managed to keep safe, tucked away in the many little drawers and cupboards in that desk. These items I have from him are more than sources of memories. It is as though there are feelings and sounds somehow contained within their very fabric, which are set loose each time I hold them in my hand.

Sad for me, Grandad Hibbitt died many years before he should have and that left a big gap in my young life. He was the father I wished I'd had. He was kind and considerate, qualities I never experienced with my father. He saw in me qualities that my father never recognized, didn't know I had within me. Don't we all want to be seen and accepted for who we are, especially by our parents?

After Granddad died, our visits to the house were less frequent. When I walked into the room that had been his study, I was shocked to see the empty space where once there had been the focus of so much pleasure. The desk of treasures wasn't there anymore. Many of the lovely, exotic contents had disappeared too. Fortunately, those items he had given me and that I still treasure, like the portable ink well, are now among my most precious possessions.

The era of happy experiences was over. It had been a heartfelt and heartwarming phase of my life, but I had those feelings and memories to sustain me, and they still do today.

Ice Cream

Would you like an ice cream?
Let's see, would I?
Would I like another one?
Smooth and creamy on my tongue.
I like that taste, so slippery smooth
Sliding down. I do approve.
What flavor though would please me most?
Vanilla, chocolate, a wondrous host
Of flavors, colors, must I choose?
By choosing one, the rest I lose.
So many there, most unknown
White, yellow, green, and brown,
Striped, chunky, nutty too.
How they're named I have no clue
I think I might try the coffee
Or should I stick to English toffee?
Chocolate chip or butter pecan
Or even Neapolitan
Moose tracks, green tea, butter brittle
Tutti fruity or raspberry ripple
Strawberry, vanilla, cookies and cream
So much choice, but I can dream.
I'll try a taste of what I pick
How tempting just to take a lick
A little spoon, a morsel sweet
A tiny taste, so petite.
A biscuit cone, packed with flavor
The perfect choice I'll always savor.
Minty green with chocolate chips

Lick it quick before it drips
On my hand, sweet as honey
Why must this pleasure be so runny?
It melts and runs and slips away
Gone for good, and I can say
That losing some makes me sad
But I am pleased with what I had.
No one can deny the pleasure
Delicious ice cream, such a treasure.

Is Mankind Born Evil?

We folks are all born evil
That's what some preachers pray
I can't believe that statement
"They've got it wrong," I say

Can our preachers be in error
With everything they say?
That's not the thing to tell us
To damn us in this way

They want to make us humble
Our spirits crushed and low
So we'll hear their words of wisdom
When they preach to tell us so

They say we're all born wicked
With evil deep within
We have to be corrected
To rid us of our sin

Where does the evil come from?
Is it there when we begin?
Derived from both our parents
Like the color of our skin?

When to this earth emerges
A newborn, without stain
Does the evil come a'calling
And settle in the brain?

Or is that tiny baby
Immune from the devil's burn
Until it meets some others
And then it starts to learn?

A baby's pure and simple
So new it knows no wrong,
Accused of being evil
Those words just don't belong

Evil's not a being
It doesn't have a life
It can't set out to harm us
And set up stress and strife

Young children learn what's evil
What's good and bad and not
But to say it starts within us
That's just a load of rot.

Walter

I push open the heavy wooden door of the Canal Turn Inn, the door with a small sign that said "Saloon Bar" in faded white letters. Inside the old stone pub, the warmth from the blazing log fire envelopes me like a soft blanket.

Several customers are enjoying their drinks and two parties of four are tucking into plates of what looks like steak-and-kidney pie as an accompaniment to their beers. I remember that the Canal Turn Inn was famous for its classic country meals, as well as for its antiquity.

As I approach the bar, I notice one man sitting in the far corner, just aside from the stone fireplace. He has a large tankard of ale on the little table beside him. Quite alone, he seems lost in the pleasures of his own thoughts while enjoying the comforts the Canal Turn provides. I cannot help noticing the clothes he is wearing, but I decide to relegate that thought to the collection of other oddities in my mind.

I study the large board behind the bar, searching for a local cask ale among the list of what is available. A young, blonde barmaid comes forward to assist me. Her smile seems quite genuine, almost as though she really is offering to help me with my choice. Sure enough, there is the beer I was looking forward to so I order a pint.

As she pulls on the beer handle and fills a pint tankard for me, I cannot help but notice the deep plunging neckline, revealing copious amounts of her anatomy, all designed to appeal to some of my male instincts. She leans forward in a deliberate gesture to display even more as I pay for my beer.

"Welcome to the Canal Turn Inn," is her opening shot.

"Thank you. But I am familiar with the pub, at least, the way it used to be thirty-five years ago. I used to live near here. But it has changed quite a bit since then."

I look around at the ancient stone walls and the collection of tools and household objects hanging from the inside of the timber roof. There's quite a museum of collectible antiques hanging up there. "Didn't there used to be a wall there?" and I point across the large room.

"Yes. It was knocked down a few years ago. Wanted to make more room for customers. There was an old storeroom behind it that wasn't needed anymore. It's made for a much nicer room, don't you think?" She smiles her well-practiced smile once more.

"Yes, of course. But tell me, and I lean towards her across the bar, mimicking her body language "The old gentleman over there in the far corner." I nod in that direction, not wanting to draw the attention of others to our conversation.

"Ah! Yes. Walter." She almost whispers the name. "Our most regular customer."

"Oh. I was wondering. He's sitting so comfortably. Looks like one of the fixtures."

"Yes, he is. Well, a temporary one. The one 'fixture' that doesn't remain here when the doors are closed each day. He comes every morning, remains all day, and leaves once the light begins to fade. He's here sun, rain, wind, or snow. Nobody can remember him ever missing one single day."

"Wow! The ultimate regular customer, hey!"

"Walter's a nice guy. Never drinks much, not as much as the Saturday night young guys, for sure. In fact, he's content with his pint tankard remaining only part full for quite a while. He never eats any of the big lunches the visitors come for. He's quite happy with some of our homemade bread and a hunk of strong cheese."

"Watches the pennies, does he?"

"No, no. I don't think it's that. And I've never seen him drunk. He's certainly not one to join in the singing that sometimes breaks out when drinkers are celebrating."

"Good for him."

She nods. "That corner's his favorite spot.... away from the noise and revelry, hidden away in his own peace and quiet. He's just ... regular."

She moves away to serve another customer with his beer but resumes her description when she's done. "At first Walter seems like a peppery old man. Looks like someone you'd not want to tangle with.... underneath, he's a man totally at peace."

I glance over at him several times, intrigued by what I was hearing. What is his story, I wonder?

He has a bulbous, pimply nose and a walrus mustache. His leather jacket, long enough to be a cloak, must trail out behind him as he walks. It looks expensive.

"Rather dramatic in his clothes," I whisper to ... Eleanor, she told me her name was.

"Yes. He comes in every morning. Flings that black hat on that peg above his head, the same peg every day. Then he settles in that chair. Orders the same beer and the same food every day. Regular as clockwork. Usually dressed the same too. Always in that black coat."

I notice the red velvet waistcoat with the gold watch chain stretched across it. He sits with his long legs stretched straight out in front, gazing into . . . who knows what, a relaxed pose, and settled, apparently at peace with everything. Customers have to be careful to avoid the pointed boots that seem so distant from the tangled mane of gray hair, the bushy eyebrows, and the jutting chin.

"He's a gentleman." She sounds quite poetic. "Underneath that aloof manner, he's courteous. He responds to greetings but he never gets into conversation with anybody. He's polite but very brief. He has a bright twinkle in his eyes, just like I imagine a leprechaun."

"Dressed like that makes me think of a pirate."

"Yes. Funny you should say that." She leaned forward again, surreptitiously. "Rumor has it that's exactly what he once was.... years ago, of course. They say he was leader of a group of smugglers. He lives just around the corner in a cottage on Canal Street.... backing directly on the canal. People say there once were men dressed all in black, in the middle of the night, carrying things through his garden and into his cottage. Course, none of that has ever been proved."

"Makes a good story, though," I tell her.

"And, there's more. When they cleared out that old storeroom behind the wall they knocked out, they found a trapdoor in the floor. Jack, the previous landlord here, told me they found some stairs going down. They started to explore the passageway underneath. Couldn't get very far because part of the roof had collapsed. But they believed that passageway was heading to the canal.... another way for goods to be brought in, especially when brandy was being smuggled in from France. Perhaps we had pirates coming in here too."

She moves away to serve another customer. Occasionally, a visitor would speak to Walter, even offer to buy him a drink. With deference and a polite smile, he always declines. He sits, he enjoys, he remains a temporary fixture.

Like Walter, I settle into my quiet space, breathing in the antiquity and the pleasures of the Canal Turn, enjoying my beer. I wonder what might have been. Visions of his life as a pirate or smuggler flash before me, as if I were a boy of ten reading Treasure Island for the first time.

Why does he intrigue me so? Is it something about the peacefulness I see in his face? Is it his clothes? He has no need to engage people in conversation; yet, he surrounds himself with people every day.

During our time on earth, there are serendipitous moments—times when people come into our lives and then leave as quickly as they came. We might take notice, often for a few brief moments, but we don't know why they captured our attention. We engage just with our eyes, facial expressions, then walk away. We don't speak, exchange words and thoughts, even when there are lessons to be learned... an opportunity for a friendship. Maybe!

Walter had certainly made me question why I was so pulled into his world. Was I imagining myself being him one day—alone, content to watch the world go by, enjoying my beer? And is that what I want for my own twilight years—being a temporary fixture?

Sarah Moreno

Summer Night in the 50s

The Fat Girl

Sugar Cookies

Sorrow

My mother was all smiles as she watched me open my sixteenth birthday present. Inside the gift wrapping was a flowered diary, encased in pink faux leather and complete with lock and tiny key.

My mother always expected great things from me. So as not to disappoint her, I started documenting my comings and goings for the first few days. Then I ventured on to confide my dreams, disappointments, feelings, and ambitions with great relish and imagination.

One morning that following summer I heard a clamoring of hooting and laughing emanating from our front porch. My thirteen-year-old sister was reading my diary aloud to the whole neighborhood. After snatching it out of her hands, I threw it in the trash.

It wasn't until many, many years later that I remembered the relief I could feel by expressing my inner self on paper. Millie, my Jack Russell terrier, and my best friend, for over seventeen years died. The grief I felt was dark and painful. In tears I believed that I could celebrate her life by writing her story. Her many adventures had the makings of a book.

How delighted I was to join Elizabeth at the Storybook House. She has mentored our group, stretched us beyond our dreams, and is the binding of this book.

As a Fifth Avenue Writer I continued to write about Millie, and I began to reminisce about all my beloved dogs. My work became a novel entitled, *You Don't Know My Jack and Other Doggone Dogs.* My intention is to finish the editing and publish this in the near future.

Presently I am working on a fictional novel based on four women who were roommates at college in the 60's. My new book will reveal their roots and choices, their joys and sorrows, as they survive personal and social expectations. My vignettes, *Fat Girl* and *Sorrow,* which appear in this book, are based on two of these characters. My goal is that my words will speak to you, the reader.

Summer Night in the 50s

Bells tinkle as I fling open the wooden screen door of the corner
    store
A few seconds from closing, I sprint across the worn linoleum floor
Throwing my nickel on the counter, ignoring fruity smells of penny
    candy in the glass case.
It is now time for the joy of reaching deep into the frosty cooler.
Hairs on my forearm rising from the cold.
Choosing my thirst-quenching treat
Tongue burning at first touch as I lap the sweet treasure.
Paper-wrapped wooden stick cannot stem the sticky stream
Trickling down my forearm and off my elbow
Drip, drip, drip!

Shouts of "Ollie, Ollie, All in Free" quieted
Outside, the street-lit game Release the Peddler is over
Deserted darkness has overtaken us all.
The short walk home stretches far ahead.
My ears strain for sounds of footsteps behind me.
My eyes scan for movement lurking in the shadows.
My thumping heart slows only when I reach my porch steps.

Through the window I see my mother in her easy chair
In the dim glow of the television
Her head nodding, pretending to watch
Her eyes fluttering up and down, and then a gentle snoring.
She's too worn to walk the stairs to face more heat
Inside the sunbaked rowhouse with its small window fan
That can only push the heavy air.

At midnight, a blaring of horns, crashing of cymbals, and pounding
    of drums
The Stars and Stripes will signal end of day's programming.
Startled at this rude awakening, Mom will then call me in.

For now, I sit with feet stretched out
My back resting against the porch post,
Inhaling the still hotness, I ponder my road ahead
Embracing this quiet time to be alone
Grateful there will be no jarring alarm clock tomorrow morning

My body at peace, melting into the night
Silence only disturbed by the roars of distant caged lions
Resonating across the reservoir waters
Representing what is to come
Knowing without knowing I am free.

The Fat Girl

After my first shower in the new dorm, I see my nude body in the full-length mirror, my face reflecting all the disgust I feel. The bright light and drops of water only enhance the rolls of fat around my waist. Love handles, shit. My thighs, my bulging upper arms, double ugh. The familiar dread of self-disgust causes my inner mantra, "fat girl, no good."

I wish for the time before my shame, my heartbreak, a time before I knew I was fat. Wanting to forget that day of infamy.

That was the day I danced ahead of my beloved grandfather, Jaja, in the bright sun. My Jaja loved to give me a day out. He would take me to the corner store and let me choose some penny candy. He told me to choose whatever I wanted and didn't care how long I took deciding between the root beer barrels, licorice, smarties, caramels, bullseyes, and many more. I always left with a bag overflowing. He would squeeze my chubby cheeks and call me his "Lenski" after we left the store.

That day the playground was almost deserted except for one boy on the swings. He gave me a quick look and then pretended I wasn't there. He must be shy, but I wanted a friend. I decided to plop myself on the swing next to him, holding the bag open so he could see the treasures inside. I politely asked him to take a piece. I hoped he wouldn't take my very favorite kind.

Then a skinny gray-haired old lady with her babushka covering her greasy hair came screaming from behind me. I was so startled the candy bag flew out of my hands.

"Don't you take no candy from nobody you don't know! Get over here! We go home! That fat girl, no good!"

Those words became embedded as if a branding iron had seared them into my soul. They hurt more than any physical damage could have done. "That fat girl, no good." Those words or some version of them keep battering at my core. Being called fatty! Or being ignored! Or not being invited to birthday parties! Or overhearing, "She has such a pretty face. Too bad she's so heavy."

My sweet Jaja, with his broken English and foreign ways, told me, "That old lady not right in the head. Don't pay her no mind."

The damage was done. I wanted to go home where no one could look at me. The torn bag lay abandoned on the ground, with candy scattered in the mud. My joy and appetite were gone.

My Jaja saw me as a healthy girl who would grow into a big, strong Polish woman, a prize as a farmer's wife in the old country. He would never understand the attraction of skinny models like Twiggy.

Nothing got better when I was in elementary school. The school work was so easy, but being smart was almost as bad as being fat. Nobody liked the "teacher's pet." One of the worst parts was gym class, where I was always the last one left when teams were chosen. It didn't matter that I was actually good at sports.

Then there was high school when the popular but dumb girls discovered I could help them with school work. They copied my answers, and I wrote essays for them. My reward was that they allowed me to sit with them at their table in the lunchroom. I wanted to feel that I was one of them, but I know they were only using me. "Fat girl, no good!" But, for me, life was better being used than being ignored. I could pretend that I belonged.

Swimming classes weren't quite as bad as I thought they would be, as long as I was in the water. I was the first one in the pool and the last one out, so I could minimize the time my body was exposed. I enjoyed the weightlessness in water and became a strong swimmer.

When undressing, comments flew around the shower room. "Look at my butt." "My sister calls me flat-chested." "My arms are too skinny." It seemed to me that most girls had issues with their bodies. But none were fat like me.

Then came my freshman year in college. My first roommate was a high school prom queen. Everything about her appearance was perfect. At first glance of me, her mouth dropped open. She backed away, turned, and left the room. One of her many friends had an empty bed, so she spent all her time there. Being alone was ok, as I was often lost in a book, and I devoted myself to my studies. No judgment if I wanted to walk around nude.

But now, in my sophomore year, I plan on it being different. I know what I'm going to do! Now it's time for my new roomies to see me in my full glory for the first time. These girls aren't popular. They're not sorority snobs. I can rule this roost.

I dress in my cotton nightdress and dance into the dorm room, parading in front of Frannie and Liz, who are working at their desks. I cup my double D breasts and belt out a song from band camp, a parody on big ears.

"Do your boobs hang low? Do they wobble to and fro? Can you tie them in a knot? Can you tie them in a bow?"

Liz and Frannie try to smile, but I can see the shock in their eyes.

Throwing my head back, I shimmy with a big finish. "Can you throw them over your shoulder like a continental soldier? Do your boobs hang low?"

"You can really dance," Liz says. Frannie just sits with her jaw hanging open.

"It's because my mother made me go to dancing school. She thought I'd lose some pounds if I got more exercise."

Hmmm. My mother, whose trim figure could still fit into her wedding dress, always had freshly baked chocolate cookies waiting for me when I got home. What kind of message was she sending me?

"My grandfather used to take me to Miss Bonnie's School of Dance every Saturday morning. I would race down the hill in front of him, skipping and singing at the top of my voice with my chubby cheeks bouncing and thunder thighs rubbing together. People would scatter out of the way."

I can entertain these skinny girls with stories about the fun I had with my Jaja, but they can never know about the dark memories I hold deep inside.

"You really have a nice voice," Frannie smiled.

These roommates have no prestige. They're not going to pose a threat. I'll be able to deal with them even if they're skinny. They are easy to shock and too innocent. I can live with them. I can use them. They can laugh with me, but they better not laugh at me!

Sugar Cookies

Wet droplets shine on sun-screened skin
Squishing sand between fingers and toes
An enticing scent of coconut
Tiny tots bring special energy
Freedom reigns at the beach.

Endless sand to be sculpted and dug
For building, destroying, spilling, dumping
Endless water for splashing, running, wading, kicking
Stomping footprints soon to be erased by lapping water

Treasures gathered in plastic buckets
Shells broken or intact
A rainbow of gleaming smooth pebbles
Bathing suits wet and gritty
Hats and sunglasses flung aside

Shouting, laughing, screaming, rejoicing
Sugar-coated bodies will eventually wear down
Sand will soon dry and sift off
Some will stick on toys as souvenirs

Looming in the future, may be cataracts and sunspots
For now, life is a day at the beach

Sorrow

A January morning, Imperial Beach, California

I wake early. The sky lightens from fog gray to pale blue. I prepare a pot of coffee and munch a piece of dry toast. The onslaught of menopause, with its slowing of metabolism, creates a battle. It seems no matter how diligent I am at watching those calories, my girth is thickening. Oh, well! Did someone write that a woman over seventy, hmmm, maybe closer to eighty if truth be told, has to have a figure of a twenty-something?

Checking to be sure, yes, I have the keys, patting the rear pocket of my baggy shorts assures me that my cell phone is with me. Making sure…that's one of those things I started doing more in the last year or so.

Leaving the condo, I silently say goodbye to my sleeping friends…. Friends since college. Grateful as always to have them in my life. I trace my way through the labyrinth of pathways, out of the gate, down the stairs and onto the sidewalk. I head to the pier.

At this dated complex directly on the beach, we enjoy spectacular views of the Pacific Ocean, especially the sunsets. This group of condos does suffer from the salt air causing corrosion to deteriorate locks and other hardware. I know that on my return I will need to jiggle and juggle the keys to unlock the entrances. A small price to pay…

I need this time alone for myself. I am struggling today more than usual. My recent loss is tugging at my heart.
An apparent homeless man shuffles by and opens the trash basket along the street. Looking for treasure, failing to find any, he passes on to the water fountain for a drink at the small municipal park. He is fully bearded and warmly dressed for the cool morning, a baseball cap pulled over his face, not paying attention to any passing by.

A memory of seeing a homeless man on the beach in Florida many years ago haunts me. He was young, wearing only threadbare shorts, and breathless from running. His smile tried to mask the fear in his eyes, but it only revealed that his two front teeth had been knocked out, marring an otherwise attractive face. As he continued running my heart sank with pity. I wanted to stop him, say you're OK, but there was nothing I could do.

Worse than that, I saw the same air of desperation and helplessness about him that I sensed in my Marco when he was a child. A foreboding gripped me then, a crippling anguish always in the background as Marco grew older.

A young man with a German Shepard is at the adjacent park. This dog disregards the plastic cone around its neck for now, as it intently sniffs blades of grass from spot to spot. His owner stands rooted, with leash in one hand, and plastic bag in the other. The ritual must be observed. Until the perfect spot is found, business can't be done.

I want to reach out and pet the dog when an image of Marco with Fina comes to mind. Unable? unwilling? to sustain a lasting relationship with the women in his life, Marco had an unselfish connection with his service dog.

More people appear, some garbed in leggings and running wear—beach walkers, runners and joggers.

A skateboarder with his backpack flashes by—more dogs, more walkers, more traffic, more sunlight.

The café now serving breakfast, smell of coffee and bacon frying.

Continuing along the Seacoast Drive... blinking lights, yellow arrows, as construction workers begin their day, breaking the peace. Diligent maintenance workers empty trash bins, hose sidewalks, sweep sand, and scrub benches.

It gets busier and lighter- the chugging bus calls for its few passengers to rush from the shelter. Hurry, we need to load, hustle, hustle. A sudden whoosh and the doors fold in. A final roar and it's gone.

A woman taps her fingers on the steering wheel of her car as she waits for the valet. He chucks the luggage into her trunk and slams it shut at beach hotel parking area. The hotel, rising from the sand with its balconies looking out to sea, is often a venue for beach weddings. The water in its towering fountain washes over granite rocks, adding a freshness and overpowering other mundane sounds.

Caw, caw, caw, a noisy bird signals its presence, heard but not seen.

None of these sights and sounds are helping to erase the images that keep appearing before me. Memories haunt me, sometimes daily.

My baseball cap is of little help against the brightness of the southern California sun. My eyes squint against the glare. My mantra before I leave this dwelling—keys, wallet, phone—must include sunglasses.

Approaching the pier, I spy a surfer gliding the waves. On the pier, fishermen are casting their lines. More surfers… seagulls drift on the breeze.

I needed no arm-twisting to agree when my dear friend invited us for a reunion. It turned out to be only a few miles north along the coast from where Marco had been camping with his service dog, Fina, last year. So near, yet I did not know it.
There is something so satisfying about the place where the ocean meets the shore and waves at us all with a consistency. Even though it does change in intensity, it will be eternally constant. Perhaps it is a consolation that even though we age and die, we go on in some form of energy. And right now, I am seeking consolation.

When I was young, the thought of death was a fearful one. Now I am the mother of a son who took his life. Tears well up at the thought of this incomprehensible event. Marco took his life, alone, in his old motorhome, so alone, that he was not discovered for days. Collected among his meager possessions was a note saying I love you, Fina. Last fall Fina had been suffering, and Marco had to have her put down. In the darkness of his grief, Marco condemned those who loved him to suffer also. Did he know how much it would hurt us? Did he know how we loved him?

Wiping my tears, I return to the condo by way of the beach. Sandals off, my bare toes sink into the sand and the cool ebbing tide as I wade quickly along. My dear friends will be waiting for me. Later in the day, after dinner, we will drink a glass of wine or two. The healing conversations will go on. Women, who have lived as long as we, have known sorrow as well as joy. There is no place for pretending.

Elizabeth Rodenz

Two Hearts

Gifts Given

Women Rise Up

Year of Loss

Travel to the Edge

Seasons Reign

Magic of Three

Mr. Penny

"Go into yourself and test the deeps in which your life takes rise; at its source you will find the answer to the question whether you must create."

Rainer Maria Rilke

At times I cannot stop my pen from flying across the page or my fingers from pressing the keys on the computer, increasing my belief that writing is what I'm meant to do at this time in my life.

For many years I had been encouraged by others to write a book, but I guess I wasn't ready. There seemed to be other mountains to climb.

When I started putting words and thoughts on paper, I realized that I had been writing all of my life, if only in my mind. All that ruminating was leading up to this time. Now, writing is a magnet pulling me into the world of words. I didn't decide to write. I write because I must.

I write to hear my thoughts, to make sense out of the minutia spinning in my head. I write to wrap my arms and head around my words to stop them from swirling. I write to feel and understand and ponder. I write to discover myself.

My first published book was a fictional tale, *Odd Ducks and Birds of a Feather,* to help others learn about personality types without wading through a list of attributes without context.

Samson and Delilah, a memoir now complete, gave me an opportunity to share the joy of loving two delightful beagles that my husband and I rescued. Along the way, I unearthed that I wanted to champion rescuing dogs more than just talking about it to others. Another book, *Josephine*, now complete, was inspired by the life of my maternal great-grandmother and the stories my mother and father told of growing up in the coal patches in western Pennsylvania. I wrote this literary novel for my own intimate purposes—to feel the reality of the stories I grew up with and to honor my legacy.

But most importantly, I wanted to expose the readers to the plight and cruelty experienced by those who made the industrial age possible. Both books are complete and will be published in 2022.

Along the way, it became obvious that many of the themes that surfaced in my writings are universal, and some of my thoughts could shake the trees and nudge people into action.

I don't write to escape or live through my characters. I leave that to others. For now, I write to create awareness of issues that either tug at my heart or injustices that must be unveiled and tackled. I write to feel and make others feel—to bring forth laughter and tears. I write so that others might imagine and wonder. I write to have an itty-bitty influence on universal themes and a collective conscience.

My poetry and short story in this book pulled me into different forms of expression, other than fictional novels and memoir, and for that, I am grateful.

Two Hearts

Tanned bare feet looking up at me
Designs left by sandal straps

Footprints in the sand
Swept away by the tide

Heartbreaking days gone by
Cleansed by the summer breeze

Dad grins like a school boy
Agog at an ocean never seen

Thrilled by the crashing waves
Spirits lightened by the wonder

Time spent together with no words spoken
Two hearts wrapped in love

Memories baked by the sun
Never to be forgotten

Gifts Given

I thanked her for her gifts of joy and strength
     So, unlike me
     I wasn't much for words
My mother silent, no words uttered
     So, unlike her
     She was definitely about words

Yet, we were more alike than different
Our love for each other, words unspoken
Bonded by the circumstances of my birth

She was the wind beneath my wings
Keen to say, "There isn't anything you can't do."
She saw in me what I could not see.

At times I cry out, wishing her back
Then tears come to my eyes and I remember
She is within me and beside me always

Women Rise Up

Once crying out for equality
Then beaten down, silenced
Settling for a few crumbs, co-opted
Becoming what THEY wanted

The deafening sound of silence
A trampled soul crying out, "What next?"

Women rise up

Patriarchy reigns with an iron fist
Shackled, under that rule
Puppeteers everywhere
Pulling the strings of your life

Who are you really?
Do you know, do you still care?

Women rise up

Reject and cast aside the praise of men
No more pleading and bleeding
For those desires never fulfilled by others
Raise your voice over a whisper in protest

Stop cutting your sisters to the quick
Saying, "choose me, not her"

Women rise up

Silence serves up greater abuses
Don't cry out, beg for that one chance
Hoping and wishing never makes it so
Sever the ties of expectations now

Say "enough," and "no more"
Walk away, never looking back

Women rise up

Decline the dictates of others
Cut the webs that entangle
Cast aside the fear of punishment

Shout out what is and what must be
And with courage, write your own song

Women—YOU MUST—rise up

The Year of Loss

Dying without loved ones near
        Heartbreak of unimaginable loss
Drowning in never-ending sorrow
        Strength and courage demanded

Crying out one more day
        Never enough time together
Death of not one but millions
        Grieving and then loneliness

Making the darkness light
        Sometimes a memory appears
Remembering loved ones cherished
        Heart and soul lightened

Bringing a smile and not a tear
        Memories never forgotten
Speaking of you, singing your praises
        You are never lost to me

Travel to the Edge

Breathing in the cool air
      Awakening my inner being
      Breathe out, breathe in
Cool breezes whispering
      Words I long to hear
      Words I need to hear

Forces pulling and pushing
      This way and that
      But I alone must decide
Desires unfulfilled
      Yearnings crying out
      Pick me, pick me

Inspiration sent from above
      Blessings of tenderness
      Igniting the flame of creativity
Another day of wonder
      Welcomed with gratitude
      Joy reigns once more

A voice shouting into the wind
      What if, what if…
      A voice pleading, "Take flight"
Forever yearning to go beyond
      Travel to the edge
      Then soar

Seasons Reign

Spring is breaking through
Melting crust of frozen earth
Breezes whispering a promise of rebirth
Ushering in tomorrow's wonder
Air crisp and fresh, stirring the soul

Snowdrops popping out in clusters
Tulips looking up to the sky
Cardinals flitting about calling their mates
Sun kissing branches of flowering trees
Delivering in abundance the colors of spring

Sun fading late in the day
Night sky glimmers like diamonds
Hot nights disturb sleep
Yet thankful for summer's beauty
Reverent taste of fruits and vegetables

Gathering outside confines of walls
Summer heat scorching the earth
Plants crying out for a drink
Rain dropping crystals of life
Quenching the thirst of dry land

Winds caressing leaves on the trees
Autumn is announcing "It's my time!"
Flowers fade as summer ebbs
No way to prolong the glory
A reminder of the fleeting nature of life

Russet and gold and red
Released and floating into the air
Crunching under my feet
Masking barren land
Brightening the earth

Cold winds blitz the landscape
Brrrr, winter is here
Snowflakes cascading down
Grabbing onto bare branches
Covering the bleakness of earth

Trees stark against night sky
A reminder of still beauty
Snow sheltering rooftops
Blanketing those within
Warming hearts until the thaw

Don't grumble because the earth is dry
Lament flowers' absence from landscape
Cry out for cooler days and nights
Wish for warmer days and nights
Gripe that the earth is no longer green

Welcome the rain that pummels the earth
See beauty in the brown of the earth
The sculpture of bare branches
Rejoice in long nights that bring quiet and calm
The snow that carpets the earth

Seasons change at their will
Colliding with each other
As one enters and another departs
Taking their place in eternal order
Reigning over our days and nights

We each have our seasons
Of birth, growth, maturity, and calm
Look around and take notice
Open your arms in welcome
Breathe in the wonder of each day

The Magic of Three

Three fluffy beds strewn around the room
All three pooches on a single one
     Squirming and jostling for comfort
     Now nestled down together

Three riveting pairs of bright eyes
Fixed on the movements of my hand
     Cupboard love or devotion?
     Maybe both, doesn't matter

Three mischievous faces tugging
At my heart, my soul, bringing a smile
     Wanting to caress them, hold them
     Every minute of every day

Three furry bodies to love and cuddle
Grinning, I kneel down to touch
     Gathering them around
     Squishing them into my body

Three doggies collapsed around me
Nestled in a bundle of warmth
     Like links of a chain, tail to nose
     Serenity tripled by love

Wishing and hoping forever together
Not one for wishing and hoping
     Wishing and hoping eternity
     Three hearts and mine as one

Mr. Penny

When I told a professor I was moving to New York City, he said, "It's fine to run away, as long as you know you're doing it."

My quick reply, "I'm not running away. I'm running to something," and somehow that rang true.

I had heard the three most difficult things to do in life are moving house, starting a new job, and severing a relationship. I decided to do all three at once. Was I up for it?

Starting a new life away from friends and family would take a bit of adjustment, so I told myself, but for me, it was a MUST. Something was pulling me to the life I needed to live. So, at thirty-nine I decided to run to something. No fear, no questioning should I. I needed to soar.

After I moved into my hotel room where I would live until I found an apartment, nothing about New York City seemed to intimidate or surprise me. The first morning as I was walking down the Avenue of the America's on my way to work, I was thrilled that I wasn't hearing any English spoken. How different from where I grew up. Within an hour, I threw myself into my work. It was where I was meant to be.

A few weeks later, Marilyn, a colleague with the publishing company I ran to, asked me to lunch. We were so different but so much alike.

She was married and believed everyone should be married. That was non-negotiable and that included me. Every time I dated anyone, which was seldom, the question the following morning, "So what do you think? Do you think he might be the one?" To her dismay, I always had a litany of reasons why it wasn't a match.

Each morning Mary, a gem of an administrative assistant and a partner in fun and work, got me coffee and a goodie at her urging. The three pennies returned to her she insisted on giving me.

Ugh.... Pennies... What am I supposed to do with them? So, I started throwing them into an empty glass vase. It was soon filled to the top, beginning to overflow.

Besides kvetching me about getting married and wearing long and flowing feminine clothes, Marilyn nudged me weekly about taking home the jar of pennies that was on my credenza.

"Someone will steal them," she would say.

"They can have them."

One evening before leaving the office, hearing Marilyn's voice, I put the pennies in a paper bag to take back to my apartment. I decided to give them to my seven-year-old nephew, thinking he would have fun counting them.

I jostled my way along 49th Street toward Seventh Avenue, holding the bag of pennies in both hands. People were coming at me from all directions. Then, someone or maybe more than one bumped into me. After all, it was New York mid-town, and a subway station was within five feet. Down went the bag of pennies, scattered all over the street. There were hundreds.

My first instinct was to walk away and leave them. But, looking at the pennies piled high, I could not do that. Someone could slip on them and fall, so I bent down and started to pick them up. People were hurrying by, stepping around me, but I held my ground. Then, all of a sudden, two men were beside me, helping me gather the pennies.

Once the last penny had been tucked safe inside my purse, I had a chance to see the two men who had been helping me. One was tall and lanky with glasses; the other short and stocky. They asked me to go for a drink and dinner. I could say because of their valiant rescue efforts, I couldn't say no. In reality, I said yes because every evening I went home to my apartment, ran out to exercise, and then had dinner alone.

There I was in New York, with everything it had to offer, and I wasn't experiencing it, so this was a chance to go to a New York restaurant and not alone. Yes, during the weekend, I went to Central Park, sometimes rode on the carousel, and watched people enjoying the park. Sometimes I went to a play and even out to dinner as a "just one." That's what they call women who eat alone in restaurants. When you walk in, the hostess looks around, and when she doesn't see anyone else, she says, "Just one," and then ushers you to a corner table.

In the three years I had been in New York, I still had no female friends to spend time with, and I had only dated one man for a period of time. I traveled most weeks. I didn't go to bars or places to meet men, and I was in my 40s. My best friend was married, as were many of my female colleagues. My male colleagues I described as three kinds of men, "Married, gay, and who cares." I was not lonely, but I spent most of my life alone or with strangers.

Throughout our getting-to-know banter, I discovered that the short one was engaged and the taller one, Mike, had just moved from Colorado to New York. Both were working for the same investment company.

Mike, the one not engaged, asked me about my work, so I shared a bit about my traveling and speaking at different conferences and workshops. I didn't give away too much, not being one to share my story again and again to those just passing through my life. It also had occurred to me that mystery in a woman can be to her benefit, so let him wonder.

We parted a few hours later, my telephone number on a piece of paper in Mike's hand, with a promise to call. I walked away thinking, "Where have I heard that before?" You see I didn't attract men. I realize now that I wasn't approachable. I had gotten out of a situation that consumed the air I wished to breathe, so I wasn't ready to jump back in, nor did I feel needy, so I didn't engage in a flirty, I'm-available way.

In the office, I was known for my adventures of meeting people, ending with an unusual twist that brought laughter and sometimes a shake of the head. After telling about yet-another encounter, a colleague chuckled, "There are a million stories in New York, and you're trying to have all of them."

So, the following morning, I told my assistant Mary about the pennies and Mike. She laughed and shook her head and named him Mr. Penny.

A few days later Mr. Penny called and invited me to see a film that weekend. Hmmm! Thinking it would be fun to hang with someone and enjoy the city, I said yes.

My mother had run away to New York when she was fifteen and had lived with a group of girls. I had run away to New York at thirty-nine and lived alone. I remembered all her stories about her friends, Far Rockaway, Central Park and ice skating, Roseland, and the Cotton Club.

That New York didn't exist forty years later, but I had yet to experience this new New York. Wanting to change that, I got caught up with the idea of having someone as a playmate.

Mike was easy to be with, and we talked about our travels and our careers and whatever hit our heads. We took walks in the park, went out to dinner, visited museums and old book stores, and took a turn at dancing. We were having fun, enjoying our time together and the sights and sounds of the city.

One night we met for dinner before I left for a business trip to the West Coast. It was his birthday, and before meeting me, he had met a friend and had a drink or two. With a Cheshire grin, he mentioned that he had told his friend about me.

"So, this friend asked me, 'How old is this woman you're in love with?'"

Love with? Who was in love?

Then he said, "How old are you?"

Mike had told me his age when he mentioned his birthday, so I knew he was thirty-three. Thinking he was the one who looked forty-two, I told him without hesitating that I was forty-two.

He was silent, so I added, "Does that bother you?"

It was about ten seconds TOO long before he said, "The last woman I dated had a sixteen-year-old son. She was forty."

He hadn't answered the question.

When I said nothing, he said, "When I first met you, I thought you were about twenty-seven."

"And your point is that I've aged well." My voice seething with anger.

He waved me off. "Then I learned you had a doctorate… learned more about your career…. I started to think you were in your early 30s."

I looked straight at him, trying not to glare. "That's nice to hear, I think."

Mike had been in an intelligence unit with the Army prior to being injured. After his dismissal, he had attended what he considered a prestigious school to get a Master's degree. I came to realize that he was trying to establish the fact that he had some smarts and that he had a prestigious position in the Army. He was always proud of his skill as a clandestine operative. Yet, all his powers of deduction had gotten my age wrong.

I rushed through dinner and left to go home and pack. I had an early flight to San Francisco the following morning. While I was gone, I called him as I promised. He was never available.

Previously when I returned from a business trip, he would call within an hour of my arrival—anxious to get together. But this time, no call. So, about three hours later, I called him and said, "What's going on?"

"I saw someone while you were away," was his quick and terse reply.

"Now, tell me something I didn't know!" was my quick and terse reply and I hung up.

By the way, I did know or I wouldn't have asked the question I did.

A few weeks later he called asking to get together. "Take control," I said to myself and then asked, "Do you have a problem with my age?"

His reply, "I don't know." Honesty! But no apology, no explanation. I was just to start spending time with him because he asked. Such arrogance!

I said in a calm voice, "Nothing will change. I'm still nine years older. I will always be nine years older. The problem with men is they think they can date someone younger, but women can't. You think you're going to age gracefully. Men get bald. They get fat, gray, paunchy, and wrinkled. When you met me, you thought I was twenty-seven."

He started to speak, but I spoke over him. "I'd like to see you when you are forty-two. Will you age as well as I have?"

Then I hung up. Whew! That felt good.

A few months later he called me around midnight. He had been out with friends and seemed to be drunk. He asked me to come over to his apartment. Did he think I inherited a stupid gene? I hung up.

Again, some months later he called and asked me to see a play. Free ticket to an impossible-to-get play, hmmm. I could say he owed me for the way he treated me, and this was one form of payment. I could say, which is more accurate, I wondered if he would talk about what happened. Why he saw someone else? Why he wanted back into my life? Maybe mention that my age did not matter....

Surprised and curious and still waiting for an apology, an explanation, something to make amends, I agreed to see him. Maybe the devil in me liked torturing him. You can look, enjoy my banter, imagine being with me, but you can't touch. Yet, I know it was more than that. I needed to see if he had the courage to explain himself. I needed to make sure that, even though I was alone and once again not experiencing New York, I would still have the strength not to fall into his arms, without thinking.

Immediately upon seeing him and trying to engage in a conversation, it was obvious nothing was there. I had shut down. I was not me. I could not let myself be me. Any signal to him that all was behind us and forgiven would not serve me well.

The play was a disaster! They were standing-room-only tickets. He hadn't told me that detail. That was another thing about him. He was a little too cheap.

He never did apologize. "I'm sorry," were not words in his vocabulary. His ego probably wouldn't give him permission. He could never admit he had a lapse in judgment or that he had made a mistake. I was just to accept that things had changed for him, and he expected to pick up where we left off. No consideration for me.

Most importantly, I had tested myself to make sure I was strong enough to walk away from him if that was what my inner being was telling me to do. After the play, I said goodnight and walked away towards the subway, leaving him standing there.

Again, he called a few months later. That seemed to be a habit he couldn't break. Maybe he thought if he gave me some time, kept calling, showing interest, we could be together again. Maybe! Or were his calls evidence that he missed me, knew he had been an idiot (or maybe they were my thoughts), and needed to find a way back into my life. Or, was it because he couldn't take rejection and wanted to prove he could get me back? No matter, it wasn't happening.

He asked to start seeing me again, and I replied, "I haven't gotten any younger. Have you gotten older?" I also added I didn't want to wake up and hear once again that he had decided I was NOW TOO-OLD. Then I hung up.

You see, before dating him, I had dated a younger man who was twenty-seven. I was then forty. I would say to him, "I'm too old for you."

He would say, "You don't have THE PROBLEM. I have THE PROBLEM. You should be saying, 'I'm too young for you.'"

He had said again and again that my age was not a factor, and I was more interesting than younger women. We had a fun romance until…. We parted because in time I discovered that he was never going to grow up. A Peter Pan without the tights. Sad though, because he was brilliant and a romantic, loving and kind. This split between us made me realize that Mike was too unfeeling, an ice cube. It is also true that I didn't reject him because I had another choice. It was because I didn't. I had discovered over the years it's more painful to be with the wrong person than being alone.

About a year later I was living in San Francisco and having a lovely life—alone. I remember saying to a friend as she probed about a man I recently dated, "I have friends. I love my work and my apartment. If this is all I'm to have, that's fine." I said it with fervor, and I meant it.

A few weeks later, Dad phoned and told me that a guy named Mike had called the house. Dad had taken Mike's number and told him if I wanted to call him, I would. Good move, Dad, not giving out my number or information.

I guessed that Mike had tried to contact me in New York and discovered my phone was disconnected. However, he knew I was from the Pittsburgh area, so he tracked down a telephone number using my last name.

His number was on a piece of paper beside my phone for several weeks. Finally, I decided to call him. In a way I was curious about his life and what had happened to him. I also needed to break his "habit" of calling me when the mood struck him. And maybe, it was also because I wanted to prove to myself again that I was strong enough not to fall into the trap of returning to a bad relationship because I was alone. Or maybe he had changed. Nay, that would make a good story, but then there's reality.

He was happy, although surprised, to hear from me. Then he told me that he was now living in Pittsburgh, and maybe we could get together when I came to visit my parents.

"Why would I want to do that?" was my quick reply. Again, I made it clear that nothing had changed and hung up. Did he think his bad behavior was something I would accept, forgive, and endure? Surely, this last call would prove to him I was not that woman.

I have known women who take men back into their lives. Maybe because it's easier. "Better the devil you know than the one you don't." I understand that.

For me, dating ranks high on my list of things I would choose not to do in my conscious moments, although there are times when I have been unconscious. Haven't we all?

Dating because we should or because we don't want to be alone. Dating because he seems nice or because we have an arm to cling to. Continuing to see him, hoping things will get better, that one day he will be the man you need in your life and he would be thankful for the person you are.

Yet, time and again, we are given proof that such relationships are fiction on a good day.

I realized at his birthday dinner that my age was a problem for him and that AGE would become a predator of my psyche. It would always be the elephant in any room we were in together.

When he looked at my face, would I be thinking: Does he notice my crow's feet, a wrinkle, a gray hair, an age spot…? Questioning over and over, my age preying on my mind.

I wasn't going to give his lapse in judgment the chance to make me doubt myself, to make me less than…. He wasn't going to get that kind of power over me.

You see, it wasn't that I had a problem with our parting. It was the way he did it, seeing someone else, negating any trust between us, and the reason he did it—my age.

I also believed our time together was past. I've noticed that women, myself included, do what I describe as "staying at the party too long." We don't give up on relationships easily—not only with men but with our hairdresser, our doctor… and other women. We keep trying to make the relationship work.

Why? The answer is different for everyone, but I was declaring my freedom from such folly.

Before running to New York, I was in a relationship I decided to end. And, I still remember my words, "I'm leaving to save myself. The fire in me is dying out, day by day. You are killing me. I want to live."

At times we all have to choose life over death, choose to live our own lives instead of doing and being what someone else prescribes for us. We have to stop letting others pull the strings. Declare we are not puppets.

Not an easy lesson and not a lesson many want to learn. Not an easy journey and not a journey many want to take. Being attached to someone, anyone, seems easier until you become conscious that it isn't.

I never heard from Mike again, but then he had no way to get in touch with me. Maybe one day he found his Mrs. Penny, but I doubt it. Psst.... and I am living happily without him.

Carole Shimko

Ode to the HOA

Broken Cookies

Mother of the Gloom

The Bride Answers Back

The Reluctant Poet

Room With a Pew

I can behave very badly. I can have affairs, stage a heist, utter obscenities, or hire a hit man to rub out my enemies. On the other hand, I can reach the heights of professional success. I can practice law or medicine, run a corporation, or sing an aria. I can achieve fame and fortune just by imagining it. I can do so many things on the page that I cannot do in real life, and it is so much fun to live vicariously through my characters!

Growing up, one of my favorite stories was "The Secret Life of Walter Mitty" by James Thurber. Mitty was a fictional character who had marvelous adventures in his fantasy life.

On the surface these escapades were humorous, but digging deeper often revealed that there was a dark side to the story. Another favorite author of mine is Daphne du Maurier, whose novels and stories are haunting in their portrayals of the conflicting aspects of human nature. James Thurber and Daphne du Maurier have influenced my storytelling in that I am inclined to use sarcasm and humor while portraying the dark side of human nature in my character's responses to life's challenges.

I write for catharsis. I am a private person and writing allows me to explore my emotions through my characters' reactions to the situations I create for them. Sometimes the situations are based on real events. This gives me an opportunity to reflect on my own behavior and feelings in such circumstances and to experiment with alternative approaches to conflict. Writing characters allows me to tell my secrets without fear, highlight my strengths without bragging, and expose my weaknesses in a safe place.

I write because it is exciting to be involved in a creative process. I enjoy the experience of honing my craft and testing my grasp of memoir, humor, drama, and poetry. The art of the craft is getting the reader to see and feel what I am putting into the words.

Finally, I write to share stories about what I have learned by living in the world. We all have stories to tell and sharing them connects us in a way that transcends cultural differences, political inclinations, and ideological constructs. Stories have always been a part of the human experience and I enjoy telling mine.

My forthcoming novel, *Broken Cookies*, examines how one woman in her golden years deals with the challenges that she faces as a member of a community, as a mother, and as a friend.

Ode to the HOA

We are the Board of the HOA
We make the rules
You must do what we say
If you stray and don't toe the line
We'll write you up
And you'll get a fine!
If we don't like you we're gonna get mean
And take your house with a nasty lien

The community docs are a great big snooze
You better read 'em or you're gonna lose
Using the clubhouse, courts, and pools
Is all controlled by our dumb ass rules
No diapered grandkids in our water
But you can wear one if you gotta
And when e-coli quickly spikes
We'll blame it on the little tykes

We don't care if you plead "No! Please!"
We're cutting down your pretty trees
"Why?" you cry as the timber falls
"Cause it's our job—and duty calls!
We're supposed to clean your gutters?
We say, "NAY!" amid the mutters
We want YOU to climb that ladder
If you fall it doesn't matter

Don't forget WE call the shots
We'll even count your flower pots

And as for all your Christmas décor
We're gonna let you know what's for
You got a wreath and a pine swag TOO?
 A violation's in store for you!
You may think we're not forgiving
It's our job—ban joyful living!

We sent you all a memo today
The annual meeting was yesterday
We know that some of you really care
But we didn't really want you there
Yes, we said we'd be transparent
By now it should be SO apparent
That what we really want to do
Is keep the facts away from you

All our contracts are really bad
'Cause we don't read 'em! Yeah, that's sad
Management tells us who to pay
They get a kickback? We can't say
Fiduciary duty? What is that?
No one said we wear that hat
When our reserve fund goes mayday
It's you, not us who will have to pay

Committees are controlled by us
Can't get on? Don't make a fuss!
Committees must be all our chums
And we pull rules out from our bums
If you're smart, we will say "NO"
Cause you'll expose what we don't know

We are going to take a stance
And wallow in our ignorance
This is how we keep control
If you want in, sell us your soul!

Go ahead-- run for election
Our cronies know about defection
If they would support your slate
They know that we'll retaliate
They have seen what we can do
And they will fear what might ensue
We will nominate from the floor
And then we will show YOU the door
To those who never tried to stop us:
Don't blame us for all the ruckus

Dear sheep, just humor us as you should
For property values, tyranny is GOOD
None of you will make a stink
You're all sedated by group think
So we know you won't jump ship
As we enjoy our power trip!
We know that we're a sorry lot
Until you wake up, we're all you've got
This is the system that we choose
Go against us—you will lose

Being on the Board is a great big plus
If we violate your rights
You cannot sue us!
Jump and shout and scream damnation
Your sorry ass is goin' to arbitration

Good luck with that
'Cause as you well know
We always win that bullshit show!

Our lawyers and management make a great team
They are really not as dumb as they seem
They have made a full-time hobby
Of bribing our state with their powerful lobby
They make sure our reps never waiver
In writing the laws to be in OUR favor
You have a complaint? Don't even begin
The system is rigged so WE always win

If you're our friend you can break the rules
You other schmucks are unlucky fools
We will nit and pick till you cry and pout
What we really want is for you to move out!
So listen dear neighbors and heed this well
HOA's are a type of hell
So raise a glass and join the cheer
Bet you are sorry for moving here!

Broken Cookies

My mother used to tell me a story about how my grandmother would go to the bakery near their house in the late afternoon to buy the broken cookies that had not sold earlier in the day. These were cheaper. Having lived through World War 1 and the Great Depression and facing life with seven children during the onset of yet another war, my grandmother had to make every penny count. My mother resented the broken cookies. She felt it was not fair that other children got the "good cookies" and she and her siblings got the "scraps."

As the oldest child, my mother had to help with the household chores and the care of her younger siblings. She used to lament that with so many kids in the family there wasn't enough love to go around. Her mother favored the "babies"—the two youngest of the brood. Mom's sister Betsy "got all the attention and affection and her brother Billy got away with murder." If there were any unbroken cookies in the bag, these two got them. My mother resented this and felt that for a mother to favor only some of her children was not fair to the others.

Years later, when we revisited these stories, I tried to appease my mother with a new perspective on these things.

"At least you got cookies. Didn't they all taste the same anyway? Didn't you admire your mother's thriftiness and appreciate her attempts to provide these treats? Wasn't it common in those days for the older children to help out with chores and parenting the younger kids?"

"Yes," she admitted. "But it still wasn't fair".

I realize now that my view of this situation did not acknowledge my mother's experience. She felt slighted, diminished, and used. But she did not articulate these feelings because she never talked about her emotions, unless the emotion was anger. Then it was OK because anger did not represent weakness in her view. If I had empathized with her at the time ("Oh mom, how awful that must have been for you"), she would have focused on her anger rather than admitting that her mother's behavior made her sad.

Over the years, her anger and resentment toward the "favored" siblings did a slow burn that manifested itself in mischievous acts of hostility on occasion. Mom told me that when her sister Betsy graduated from high school, grandmother asked her to iron Betsy's graduation dress. "Accidently on purpose", she scorched the dress and ruined it. I said, "That was really mean." She sighed through a wicked smile and replied, "I know."

I was conflicted about my relationship with Aunt Betsy. She was my godmother, and she was often kind and giving. On occasion, she would bring me a small gift or a sweet.

But she was also a taker—and she would take greedily. When the family assembled at my house for Christmas, we knew Aunt Betsy had arrived when someone yelled, "Hide the cookies!" That was because one year, while we were playing a game in the living room, Aunt Betsy emptied all the cookies and desserts into shopping bags that she had stashed in her purse and ran them out to her car. Eventually, I did start hiding the cookies. But she always found them and put them in the trunk of her car when no one was looking.

She also fancied herself a gardener and liked to propagate plants with "cuttings". Once, while I was walking her to her car after a visit, I burst out, "What the hell happened to my garden?" She waved me off with a flutter of her hand. "I just took a few cuttings", she said with annoyance at getting caught. My entire garden was leveled to the ground. And, when I went back into the house, I saw that she had taken all of the spaghetti sauce that I had prepared for the freezer. ALL of it. When she died, I had so much repressed anger that I was minimally sad.

One day, my grandmother told my mother to repair a hole in Billy's swimming trucks. She sewed the leg openings together, "accidentally on purpose". I was at my grandmother's house when Billy ran in screaming that he fell over in the woods near the swimming hole while trying to put on his trunks. He was afraid that he was "going to get poison ivy on his bum." I took a cue from my grandmother who laughed so hard she had tears in her eyes, and I laughed too. This made him even more angry, and he stomped out of the room, yelling that I was a "brat who better look out."

I was six at the time and he was sixteen. I remember that I was not upset by this incident because in my child's mind I thought he was stupid and that someone who was that stupid could pose no threat. And he didn't look threatening. He was chubby with a round rosy face and a mop of blond hair that he kept pushing out of his pretty blue eyes. But I didn't like him then and I didn't like him after we both grew up.

As an adult, he continued to behave like a spoiled punk. He couldn't hold down a job because he would refuse to do tasks that he felt were beneath him. His wife left him because she said he was more like a child than a husband. We dreaded his presence at family parties because he would demand his favorite foods and expensive vodka. The last time I saw him was at a funeral and he was already drunk at 10 o'clock in the morning.

When he died, I thought, "What a waste of DNA. At least he's out of the gene pool." I did feel guilty about feeling that way, but I could not conjure up any redeeming qualities of his to mitigate my guilt.

My mother often said that Betsy and Billy were just two more broken cookies that she had to learn to accept. But her purposeful "accidents" helped her to cope.

"Accidently on purpose" became code in our family for passive-aggressive revenge in response to little injustices or unfairness. It was a prank carried out with humor or malice, depending on the situation and the perpetrator's mood. With my mom as a role model, I was learning how to channel anger and outrage into these pranks to cover up my emotions so as not to appear weak or "mushy"—her favorite word for emoting.

The notion of fairness permeated my mother's behavior toward me and my brother. If I needed a new coat, he got one too. If he wanted a new bike, I got one too. We had exactly the same things in our bedrooms—a twin bed, a dresser, a desk, a TV, and a telephone.

We didn't have a lot of money. In those days, my father earned one hundred dollars each week as a house painter. But my mother was able to manage that money so that we kids were never without necessities and even some luxuries. I once saw her counting slices of deli meat so that it would last for the whole week's lunches, making sure that everyone got the same amount. And she put money aside for one winter so that she could buy us an above ground pool when summer came.

One day, there was a knock at the door and when my mother opened it, there was a woman with a tall boy standing there. "Hello", the woman said "I'm Ellen and this is Buddy."

"Yes", my mother replied. "Wait here. I'll be right back" and she went to get her purse. This woman and the boy came by about once every month and mom always had them wait on the porch while she fetched her purse.

When I was in high school, my mother finally explained these visits. My father had had a "fling" with this woman when he got out of the army, and they had a son. The woman needed help with child support, and she approached my parents. My mother said she would take care of it out of her budget. When I asked her why she agreed to do this, she said, "That kid was the spitting image of your dad and they needed help. Children come first before anything else. We have a little to spare. It's the fair thing to do."

Once, my mother returned from a doctor's visit in tears. She blurted out "I have Type 2 diabetes. This is so unfair!" Then, the very next day, she said, "This happened because I eat too many sweets. This is not going to get me down. If I lose weight, I won't need medication." And she went on a diet, lost 50 pounds and boasted "No insulin for me!"

My brother and I were stunned at how tiny she was after this weight loss. She stood at about five feet, but always had what we called a "sturdy presence." My brother liked to tease her by lifting up her new diminutive frame saying, "Look! A new piece of furniture!" He would carry her from room to room exclaiming, "This looks better in here, don't you think?" She would protest loudly, proclaiming, "Something accidentally on purpose is going to happen to you!"

After the weight loss, her hair fell out. She didn't lament about it after the doctor told her it was probably permanent. She went to a wig shop and came home with a wig. "Now I can have curly hair when I want to," she said, fluffing up the tresses in the hall mirror. Upon watching this my dad said, "You look a lot like Queen Elizabeth!" The resemblance was remarkable. She replied, "Well thanks a lot, Bud. The Queen is so damn ugly. I'm going back to the store for a different model."

Mom needed several joint replacements because of severe arthritis. She blamed this on her mother's poor nutrition during the wars and Depression. She said, "It's my mother's fault I have such bad bones. But I guess there was nothing she could do about it. Anyway, now I'm like the bionic woman!" She uttered this gleefully when setting off alarms in airport security lines.

As the years went by, there were more broken cookies for mom. After 37 years of marriage, my dad died at the age of 73. Mom was only 56 years old, and she was devastated. "Not fair that he was taken from me so soon, but at least I had the love of my life for a while. A lot of people don't get to have that." Her eyes were glistening at the funeral, but I didn't see her cry. From then on, there were no more parties or celebrations in her house—no more Christmas trees, Easter baskets, or birthday cakes. All family celebrations were moved to my house, and she remained in mourning for the rest of her life.

Then, one day, I found a notepad on her desk entitled "Things to say on the phone to the kids". There was a page for the current day of the week and the date. There was a list of current events topics. A list of family birthdays. And notes from previous phone calls. She was experiencing the beginning signs of dementia and she didn't want my brother and me to know. When I saw this, I thought, *This was the thing she was most afraid of, 'Losing her marbles,' as she would put it. How unfair!*

What is fair? We have no control over what life throws at us and often, it is not fair. The "cookie thing" (as our family used to call it) represented life's ups and downs for my mother. When someone appeared distressed, my mother would ask, "Someone break your cookies?" My mom's philosophy for dealing with broken cookies was, "If you can do something about a bad situation, then do it. If you can't do anything about it, then learn how to cope and stop whining."

Once I was in a bad car accident and my mom sat near my bed in the Intensive Care Unit while we were waiting to learn if I had broken my back. I had just given birth to my first child, and I was on the verge of hysteria. My mother said, "Can you do anything about this right now?" When I said, "Of course not", she replied, "Let's wait to hear what the doctor has to say, then we'll make a plan." This was so empowering that I immediately calmed down. And, she said it with such compassion that I felt everything would be ok with her by my side.

After she said these things, her eyes became moist, and she started to fiddle with the TV remote. She turned her back to me and faced the TV so that I would not see her cry. We never saw each other cry because neither of us would allow it. My mother always said that displays of emotion were "mushy". She would say, "Don't dump your feelings on other people. Then they have to deal with them, and it makes people uncomfortable." She also believed that one must "conquer" fear and anxiety. "Conquer" was one of her favorite words. Whenever my brother or I faced a difficult situation, she would point her finger in the air and command, "Conquer it!"

Mom taught me and my brother how to cope with life's challenges and how to infuse humor and kindness (and mischief) into dealing with problems. Because my brother and I were treated fairly and there was no favoritism, we were never competitive and became very close. We remain close as adults. He protects me because he is "the guy," and I take care of him because I am "the big sister."

Mom taught me how to be a good mother to my own son and daughter by being fair and by "spoiling them sweet" (lots of love) rather than "spoiling them sour" (no discipline). My two children now say that they grew up secure knowing that they were loved equally. They are good friends and confidants. And they are terrified on rare occasions when they see me cry. They say that "if mom is crying, something horrible is happening—she never cries." I do cry sometimes. I just don't let anybody see it. I am still working on expressing my emotions, even if it is "mushy."

My children adored my mother, and they say they know when her spirit is hanging around them because they smell Estee Lauder perfume that she always wore.

My mother eventually succumbed to dementia at the age of 81, despite her valiant and creative attempts to cope with it. Before that happened, however, she gave a whole cookie to everyone she encountered.

Mother of the Gloom

My Golden Boy's about to marry
I really wish that he would tarry
I'm his mom; I know what's best
It's not *this* girl; she failed the test!

The way she is—it's not enough
I'm not convinced she's got the stuff
To make him as happy as he can be
What can I do to make him see?

Although he tells me "She's the one"
I don't believe she's for my son
I wish that I could wave a wand
And toss her back into the pond

My sage advice he did revere
But now he says, "Don't interfere."
"I've got this, mom, it's not your choice."
In this I'm not to have a voice

I do believe he is the best
I think he should pursue the quest
But off he goes, my pride and joy
She's captured him--my Golden Boy

My task is clear; let go of strife
To be a part of his new life
Ok, I get it—I won't mope
I've got no choice; I'll learn to cope,

But I won't like it.

The Bride Answers Back
To the Mother of the Gloom
From the Pending Daughter-in-Flaw

You think your boy is such a prize?
You see yourself as sage and wise?
Well, I could say a thing or two
You really haven't got a clue!

I'll tell you this right off the bat
Your Golden Boy is not "all that"
He does some things that make me mad
And oftentimes he makes me sad

You've taught him that he does no wrong
This makes it hard to get along
He's never learned to give and take
And that's your fault—a big mistake!

Say whatever; I don't care
I'm not going anywhere
Cause he's my love and I won't budge
You shouldn't be so quick to judge

So go ahead and wave your wand
I'll not go back into the pond
You'll see when all is said and done
You must accept I love your son

I won't give up; I'll fight for him
I love your son; it's not a whim
Don't rue the wives he could have had
In time you'll see I'm not so bad

So there!

The Reluctant Poet

A poet I will never be
The very thought disquiets me
Don't poets need to bare their souls?
My writing looks to other goals

My secret thoughts must stay just that
Protecting them is where I'm at
I won't tell you who I am
You might see past the flimsy glam

A private person thru and thru
I won't reveal myself to you
Poems reveal us bit by bit
It's not for me from where I sit

You might decide there's nothing there
For me that thought provokes a scare
Because you see, I'm not all that
My back does not deserve a pat

My company you'll not abide
At one good glimpse of my dark side
Bare myself to your critique?
Then say good-by to my mystique

I'm not inclined to let you see
My faults and insecurity
So, I will never write a poem
I'd rather write the greatest tome.

A Room with a Pew

"Well, I must say, I've never actually got it on in front of the Blessed Virgin Mary. This will be a first," Devin said upon surveying our room at the Country Inn.

I smiled and said nothing. I was hoping she—the Virgin Mary—would not be a problem. People our age have enough impediments to romance without a Catholic guilt trip. And, anyway, we had both abandoned Catholicism many years ago, so maybe she would leave us alone.

I had just returned from several weeks in England and Devin suggested that we get away for a quiet weekend to reconnect. I told him, "I'll take care of it. I'll find a nice romantic place where we can spend a glorious weekend just enjoying each other".

After a quick Internet search for Bed and Breakfast establishments in the countryside, I found the perfect place. It had rave reviews on Yelp and was a short drive to one of our favorite restaurants. "You will love it," I said.

So, we ventured out on a sunny Friday morning in great anticipation of relaxation, great food, and good snuggles. We drove for over an hour and should have been approaching the Inn according to the GPS, but alas, no B and B in sight.

"Let me call the place for directions, it can't be far," I offered. A very pleasant woman answered the phone and chuckled in response to my request for the location. "Everyone drives right past this place," she said. We followed her instructions and within minutes we were facing a sign that said ROBERTSHAW COUNTRY HOUSE and (in very small print) BENEDICTINE MONASTERY. "You can't be serious," Devin said. "Well, we're here. Let's check it out," I replied.

I rang a doorbell that sounded like the round metal bell with the finger lever that I had on my bike as a child—staccato metal screeching summoned someone to the door. A tiny gray-haired woman with a crooked smile (a remnant of a stroke or Bell's Palsy, I thought) struggled to pull open a large wooden door, and panted, "You must be Charlotte and Devin. Come in, come in."

She led the way with a limp and a cane since one hip was higher than the other and we followed her into a large living room decorated with oriental rugs, red and green velvet sofas, and a large portrait of an elderly man over a crumbling brick fireplace that had been painted white. There were piles of books everywhere—on coffee tables, end tables, and the floor. It reminded me of an opening scene in an Agatha Christie novel and I felt comforted and quite at home.

"My name is Molly and I volunteer here. I do household chores and make breakfast for the guests. Mother Superior will be here shortly to see you to your rooms." Rooms, as in plural of room.

Devin was behind me, and I resisted turning around. I feared that if we made eye contact, I would erupt into uncontrollable laughter, and I did not want to offend Molly. Then, the front door opened.

The swishing of the movement of voluminous fabric and the clinking of beads against metal conjured up the anticipatory anxiety provoked by such acoustics in the hallways of my parochial grade school. Mother Superior was in the house.

My mouth went dry and I was sure I was having heart palpitations. In a flash of Woody Allen inspiration, I thought how darkly funny it would be if I dropped dead from fright right at Mother Superior's feet. "Good morning," she said. "You may call me Sister Constance." The plethora of black fabric did not hide her corpulence and her round pink face was entombed by a white board-like structure over her forehead and a stiff white collar that squeezed her chin up to her ears. A long black veil hung from this construction, and it looked so tight that I expected her eyes to pop right out of her head. Yet, she seemed very comfortable in this contraption, even though it was the middle of August.

She handed me a small card. "Here you go," she said. "The Wi-Fi code. A hundred years ago, the guests wanted a roof. Then, they wanted windows. Now everybody wants Wi-Fi. What's next?" She giggled and shook her head.

"I'm going to show you around, then I'll take you to your rooms." Rooms. Plural. So much for the romantic weekend. I sensed Devin shuffling behind me. I still lacked the courage to turn around and face him.

She beckoned us to a door at the end of the Agatha Christie living room. This led to a long hallway that had twenty cells, as she called them, on each side. Each cell had a single bed, a chair, a small window, and a black crucifix on the wall. Devon whispered in my ear, "What, no mini-bar?" Then he pinched me on my derriere.

A loud "Oooh," escaped from me.

"Yes, this is our gift shop," Sister said. "I'm so glad you like it. It's honor system. Take what you like and pay me later."

Next, she led us into a large chapel. "You can come in here anytime you want," she said. "Vespers at four o'clock. Devin remarked, "Oh good, I could use a drink." She ignored him. I was ready to kill him. "Now, let's get you to your rooms." Rooms, plural.

We went back through the living room, and then Sister led us up a carved wooden staircase. "I put you in the suite. I think you will like these rooms," she giggled. She opened the door to a large sitting room with a plush sofa and chairs. We walked down a short narrow hallway and peeked into a modern bathroom with a Jacuzzi tub and shower. "Here is the bedroom," she said, opening another door. And, there it was. At the foot of the king size bed. A huge framed poster of the Blessed Virgin Mary.

Suddenly, I heard church bells ringing. "Oh, that's my cell phone alarm," Sister said. "Time for Vespers." She started to leave, then turned around with an impish grin. "There's vodka, gin, and Lillet in the kitchen, if you prefer the other kind of Vespers. And, don't mind Mary. She's seen it all."

And with that, I almost fell to my knees.

Sarah Holler

Enjoying the Cruise

Senses of Majorca

Winter Quiet

Missing Teeth

First Encounter

"If there's a book that you want to read, but it hasn't been written yet, then you must write it."

Toni Morrison

My writing has taken many twists and turns over the years. Poems scribbled on scraps of paper as I tried to come to grips with challenges life threw me. Stories written only to be shoved back deep into a desk drawer.

My childhood was always filled with words. Books covered every flat surface in our home. My father taught English and often recited poems to us on family trips.

My brother and I liked the sound of his voice, and his unique animations captured our attention, connecting us in ways we seldom experienced with him.

Our father encouraged us to play words games to entertain ourselves. Our favorite game often involved ants or lima beans as the main characters. The plots always centered around criminal trials complete with a jury. Subjects were then put on trial and found guilty of their crimes. We spent hours during the summer months concocting different versions.

Due to the influence of my Father, the last several years have been spent writing poems about places or seasons which are dear to my heart. Recently my writings have centered around my growing up years. These stories have allowed me to rewrite a different ending to some painful moments in my life. Childhood was not a joy filled adventure, quite the opposite. Writing allows me to deal with these moments. I write for the freedom and growth I find in these finished pieces. This has been both healing and empowering.

My Aunt Lib has also had a huge influence on my writing. I remember talking with her about her writing journey. My aunt, at the time in her nineties, was living in an assisted living facility. Aunt Lib shared how thrilled she was the facility newsletter featured her poems. The delight and pride she took in this made me realize what a gift writing imparts to the writer as well as reader. My cousin has shared with me poems her mother had written when she was only eight years old. Such a wonderful way to peek into the life of a child in the early 1900s. My aunt passed away but has been able to share so much in the writing she has left behind.

Writing, for me, is about the joy of using words. Can I convey, to the reader, what I see in my head? Can those words pull up emotions, bring the reader into the story? Can I paint a picture using words I choose. The need to find just the right words keeps me writing. I often imagine my aunt sitting close by encouraging me to keep going when the words do not always come to me.

I have discovered that writing can evolve into a community of writers bringing me great joy. I am thankful to the Fifth Avenue Writers as each has encouraged and cheered me on toward writing poetry and stories, I am proud to share.

Enjoying the Cruise

Hands joined
Neither noticing arthritic knuckles

Moving slowly past the nurses' station
Eyes twinkling through clouded lenses

Slow progress
Tap, tap, cane hitting tile

A smile forms
Glancing at him, her face glows
Long years, short years

She hums
Words long forgotten

She turns to him
Enjoying the cruise?
She whispers in his ear

Eyes moist, he turns
Adrift in a memory
Yes, he whispers

Senses of Majorca

Sweet, sour, tickling my nose
Orange marmalade
Orange marmalade!

Freshly brewed coffee
Briny sea scents
Joining the party

Breathe in, breathe out

My eye memory sees
Blue cloudless sky
Seagulls gliding on unseen currents

Breathe in, breathe out

My eye memory sees
Azure ocean kissing the shore
Sea urchin shells resemble pincushions
Octopus moving with snake-like legs
Bright orange starfish creeping

Breathe in, breathe out

Eye memory sees
Majorca

Winter Quiet

The snow falls
Each flake its own design.
Turning green grass glistening white
Street light bounces off the ground.

The world becomes quiet
Sound muffled through earmuffs.
Sound softened, light as snow continues its descent.

Air crisp, sharp, breathed in cleaner.
Traces of tar, car exhaust banished.
Our lungs breathe in crispness
We are renewed.

Footprints mark our journey.
Snow erases a walkers' existence.
Nature attempts to recreate an unspoiled landscape.

Tree branches heavy with snow bend
Take a final bow in the snow performance.

Missing Teeth

The dry, yellowing scotch tape gives way as I lift the lid of the box. Photos spill out onto the floor as the box comes apart. I bend to pick them up when one particular photo catches my eye.

The man pictured is wearing a well-worn corduroy jacket with leather elbow patches, a pressed white shirt, and a striped tie. Knowing him as I do, he probably hopes this will peg him as a Greenwich Village author or playwright. No three-piece suit for him. God forbid someone takes him for an uptight commuter-riding stiff heading into New York to a stuffy job.

He is perched, leaning toward the photographer, on an oak desk covered with coffee ring stains and initials etched in by his students. He has a slight smile playing across his lips, probably saying to himself, "Oh, don't I look wonderful?"

To those who do not know him as well as I do, it appears he's connecting with the photographer, but I know better. The look on his face is one of familiarity, so I wonder who the photographer was. One of his many admiring junior high students? Perhaps a photo meant for the yearbook? Someone who more than liked him? He, she? That's anyone's guess.

This man is my father. His name is Charlton and look out if you call him Carl. He taught English in the junior high I attended. An arrangement I was not happy with. His very presence overshadowed me, so each day, I felt myself becoming less and less visible.

The beginning of each school day excited my father. He always smiled when telling us with great pride how his students, in turn, greeted him with smiles and stories of their latest escapades. I often imagined him as an actor gearing up for opening night.

Seeing this photo of Dad brings back the memory of an event that was life-changing for me. The year was 1959.

It began one morning when I walked past his classroom and noticed him standing by the open door. He watched his students entering the room the way a mother looked at a favored child. I remember wishing he would look at me that way.

Later that morning, I was paged over the intercom to come to the office. As I came around the corner, somewhat out of breath, I saw my father. "What ... what's wrong?" I shouted, irritated he had dragged me out of my favorite class.

He was scowling, and his eyes were glaring at me. "Hanna. I nee' ya' to 'alk 'ome, git m' brid.. of' te' 'ink and brin' it 'ack 'ere. Right 'ow."

I had trouble hearing him, and the words coming out of his mouth were barely recognizable.

"Na' gi' goin'."

"I can't understand what you're saying." I tried to hold back my delight. He had forgotten his teeth.

"Dad, you're talking like you have a mouthful of cotton? Why did you call me down here?"

He stood there shaking his head, lips tightly pursed, as he tried again. "I nee' ya' to go 'ome a' git my brid."

"Dad, I still don't get it. Why are you talking like this? I don't know what you want me to do! I've got to get back to class before I get into trouble."

I turned to head back to class, trying not to burst into laughter.

Dad, now with his lips no longer glued together, said, "I want you to go home and get my bridge."

I stood there staring at him, my mouth worked overtime to keep from laughing. "Oh, I see! You don't have your teeth!"

"Right." At this point, Dad lost his patience. "Now quit talking before someone hears you and get going." I took a deep breath, smiling like I had swallowed some feathers, and headed towards the school's front door. As I turned the corner, a student bumped into me, causing his books to fly out of his arms. "Sorry," I said as I bent to help him collect them.

He looked up, "Hey, aren't you Mr. B's daughter? Wow!"

Great! Yet again, I have no identity other than being Mr. B's daughter. Just once, I would like people to see me. Just once, I would like people to say, "Oh, you're Hanna, the modern dancer." "Oh, Hanna, I remember watching you dance on stage and wishing I could move the way you do. It looked like you were having so much fun."

My father's bigger-than-life personality always seemed to take over. I wanted to scream, "No, I am Hanna! Not Mr. B's daughter! Hanna! Get it? Hanna!"

"How great it must be to have such a cool dad! All the kids love him! He lets us play records in class. Not like the other teachers. He's just so cool."

Yeah, well, you don't have to live with him. Shaking, my cheeks on fire, I turned away without saying a word.

The father I knew was not what the world outside saw. The minute he walked into our house, the cool teacher mask disappeared. Every evening after school, he headed to the liquor cabinet, and we soon heard ice clinking in his glass. Sometimes, he said hello, but most often just went upstairs until it was time for dinner.

As I raced towards the exit door, I remembered a night when I was eight years old. I was put in charge of watching my brother while my parents went to a cocktail party at the neighbors.

My brother and I had both gone up to bed. I heard the wind scraping a branch against the porch roof. I sat watching shadows crawl across the wall, my breath becoming shallower as I saw what appeared, in my eight-year-old's eye, a ghostly figure. My whole body was frozen in place as I watched the bizarre shape floating closer to the window. I felt terror building inside me as I ran to the phone and called my parents.

I dialed the phone. "Mrs. Shipley, I want to talk to mom."

"Wait a minute," she replied. I waited, hearing sounds of laughter and music working its way through the phone line.

My mother shouted, "What's the matter?"

"Come home? I'm scared. Someone is trying to get into the house," I whimpered while trying hard not to cry.

"Ok, we'll be home in a few minutes," she said.

I relaxed as I waited for my parents. The night sounds didn't seem quite so scary now, so I went back to my room. Asking my parents to come home turned out to be worse than the sight of a ghostly shadow.

I heard our front door open as my parents returned. I knew there would be trouble as I listened to their voices getting louder. I lay still, not making a sound, hoping my mother would come into my room to see if I was ok. She did not, but then why did I even think she might? It's still difficult to admit that both of my parents had the title of Mom and Dad.

Their arguing continued and seemed to get louder. Then I heard my father stomping his way to my room. There was a loud crash as a chair hit my bedroom door, and my father started yelling. He was angry, blaming me for the reason he had to leave the party early. The reason he was no longer center stage, continuing to hold his audience's attention. I began to crawl down deeper under the covers, trying to hide, waiting for him to go back to his room. At some point, the whole house was quiet.

The next thing I remember is opening my eyes. It was morning.

The smell of coffee wafted up the stairs letting me know my parents were in the kitchen. I tiptoed down to the playroom, hoping not to be noticed. I almost made it before my mother called, "Hanna, where are you going? Come in the kitchen for breakfast."

I sat down at the table and began to eat, and my shoulders slumped, my eyes focused downward on my food. I realized last night was never going to be acknowledged, let alone discussed. No apology for the chair-throwing. No concern for how scared I was.

This was the father who lived in our house. This was the man all the kids at school thought was so cool. If they only knew.

As I continued to walk home, the sound of a horn startled me. I stopped just in time to see a car buzzing by me, realizing tears were streaming down my cheeks.

The minutes it took me to cross the street and walk the shortcut home, I noticed my breathing return to normal. As I walked, it dawned on me this errand had given me a great way to blow off the rest of the school day. School was something I endured, so any chance to escape was welcomed. This revelation slowed me down to a snail's pace.

After all, what was the big hurry?

Dad would have to wait. Humm, here was an opportunity for me to throw a monkey wrench into his day. See how he liked it. Since I was on an errand for Mr. B., no one would question where I was.

On the way home, I was getting angrier. Then I started to laugh out loud. Humm, I wondered what would happen if I didn't go back with "Dad's Bridge?" The more I thought about this, the better I felt. I began to sing, "We Shall Overcome."

That day was the moment! I would become the Disobedient Daughter! I liked the sound of that!

I giggled and noticed my stomach had filled with bubbles jumping for joy. What would the kids say? Amazed, I thought and could hear them, "Hey, you know Mr. B's quiet daughter had the nerve to leave school and not come back. I never thought she had that in her."

These thoughts were flying around in my head, and I liked them. I would become known as bold and daring. What a switch that would be.

These thoughts encouraged me, and I hatched a plan. Opening the front door, I headed to the kitchen and grabbed the phone. Yes, I was going to do it. The excitement gave me courage I never knew I had.

"Hi Mrs. Jones, this is Hanna. My father asked me to pick up his bridge. But on the way home, I fell and hurt my leg. I will not be able to return to school today. Please let my dad know I will not be coming back with his bridge."

"Bridge? What are you talking about? Bridges?"

"No, No, my father left his false teeth on the sink in our bathroom. I was on my way home to get them when I fell. Just let him know I won't be back."

That felt good. Wow, I finally refused to disappear.

My entire body was smiling with delight as I leaned against the counter. The vision of my dad spending the day talking out of the side of his mouth was heady.

Mrs. Jones would tell him the bad news that I won't be back. I wondered if it would be too much for him, and he would drive home. This thought moved me into action, still smiling.

I headed upstairs to gather an Ace bandage. After all, I needed to look as if I sprained my ankle or something. Maybe I could play it up and slap a huge bandage on my elbow.

The day I disobeyed my dad, I knew I would no longer allow myself to be invisible, that I was becoming my own person, a person he would have to reckon with and may not like. I delivered a blow to his ego and what started as a way to get back at him began my journey to claim who I wanted to be.

I realize now "missing teeth" stood for so much more in our family. They symbolized the missing moments in our home—moments of laughter, compassion, joy, caring, and unconditional love.

First Encounter

Matt puts out his thumb to hitch a ride home from high school. He noticed the sun was creating lacy patterns along the road like the doily on his mother's dressing table. The walk home, if he didn't catch a ride, took about one hour. He walked along graceful and fluid as a male dancer.

Several cars had slowed but then moved on. He felt they were teasing him, offering a ride only to step on the gas, leaving him alone again.

He liked to hitchhike. Every driver had an interesting story. Matt felt his world expand with each one. Maybe today, a city driver would stop and share stories of eating in a fancy restaurant or going to the theater. Better yet, a writer. Matt fancied himself a writer. Wouldn't it be great to catch a ride with someone like Hemingway? Now there was a man who had really traveled and experienced life.

The mayor of his town stopped once, and as Matt hopped in, he began droning on about his upcoming election campaign. The mayor was oversized and spoke with a cigar glued to his lips. The cigar smoke reminded him of the burn barrel his mother used to dispose of their garbage. Matt had trouble staying awake during that ride. That was NOT one of the better rides.

Beep, Beep. Matt jumped as he realized someone was going to stop and offer him a ride. He ran over and opened the passenger door. He ducked his head and looked in. The man gave him a slow smile, "Going to Hamilton?"

"Yep."

"Ok, then hop in."

Matt got in, and as he did, the scent of Old Spice teased at his nose. He glanced sideways, trying to study the man without seeming to

stare. Surely, he was a professor at the college. Loafers' spit and
polish clean, trousers pressed, and not a wrinkle in sight. He had
horn-rimmed glasses which did not hide the blue eyes that drew
Matt in. Brown hair tousled casually but with great care gave him
a somewhat exotic appearance. Yes, decided Matt, he is a
professor.

"Hey, my name is Steve."

"I'm... I'm Matt," he stammered.

Steve asked Matt questions about school, his family, and
what were his favorite sports. "Well, actually," Matt answered, "I'm
more interested in books, acting, and art."

Steve laughed. Matt liked the sound of his laughter and
found he wanted to make the professor laugh again. This WAS one
of the more exciting rides, and he didn't want it to end. He liked
talking to the professor.

"Hey Matt," Steve said. "How about ice cream? We can
take it to a park nearby."

"Yes," Matt said, smiling shaking his head enthusiastically.
Wow, this guy is great. So different from the men he knew in town.
Those men didn't know anything about books or poetry. Steve had
been talking for at least twenty minutes about Robert Frost, who
happened to be one of Matts' favorite poets.

The professor interrupted his thoughts. "Do you want
chocolate or vanilla?" Matt blinked when he realized they had
reached the ice cream parlor.

"I'll have chocolate."

"Chocolate it is," said Steve. The professor ordered, and as
he handed the cone to Matt, their fingers touched briefly. They
hopped back into the car and headed to the park.

Steve slowed the car to a stop. Matt looked around,
surprised he had never been here before. He realized they were
alone. Matt noticed the professor watching him as he finished his

cone. Steve then turned toward the young man as his arm crept out and placed it around Matt's shoulder. Matt wasn't quite sure what was going on, but he knew what he was feeling. He never felt this way with the girls he had dated.

At sixteen, Matt had no idea that this moment with the professor had changed his life. A life that would force him to live in the shadows forever.

He never saw the professor again. Years later, he would recall that moment the way one remembers a first love.

Epilogue
Daisy, Zoey, and Me, Emma, and the Fifth Avenue Writers

I wake up, crawl out of bed, and stretch my back. "It's Wednesday again," I yawn. "Those people are coming again."

Zoey wags her tail. "I knew you could tell time, Emma, but I didn't know you could keep track of the days of the week."

"When you've been around as long as I have kid, you've got… what humans call insight."

Daisy, still trying to wake, shakes her body, mustering the energy to rise up. She's happy her mistress no longer calls her Lazy Daisy, but she knows she'll never lose the name, Crazy Daisy. She's also known as the "poppet."

"Well, I love Wednesday," says Daisy, her tiny body almost moving. "Someone comes and pets me, then someone else arrives and pets my head—they're all so happy to see me."

"What about me," grumbles Zoey. "They like me too."

"Yea, but I know I'm their favorite. They let me hop on their laps and coo over me."

"Well, I can't jump like you can, but I know they like me."

I look over at the two and grumble. "Stop that fussin' you two. I'm their favorite. You two are just pushy. That's why you get all the attention. Get movin'. It's time for food."

You see I'm what my mistress calls "a foody." My master says I'm "the nagger." All names are compliments to my discriminating taste.

I'm not only the oldest, I'm the calmest—an old crone. Daisy is crazy but in a good way. Zoey got her name from the Greek word for life. She is indeed lively.

Well, enough about us. I want to tell you something about the Fifth Avenue Writers. Having spent several years listening to their stories and hearing comments, as the eldest of the three of us, I'm the most qualified to say something about the writing group that meets at our house.

Usually Sarah #2 (we have two Sarah's and she joined second) arrives first with a cheerful greeting. She's always early because she lives a block away. She's thrilled to be part of a group that doesn't mince words and is vested in each other's writings. Although I think that could be said of all of them. She started writing a story with a beagle in it (I believe because she fell in love with us) but abandoned it for other stories. I hope she gets back to it. I can help her, making sure the beagle behaviors she writes about are authentic. She has a cat, and I want to make sure she doesn't get confused.

Joanne and Sarah #1 arrive next and always together, sharing a ride every week. Sarah loves dogs. I think she would take Daisy home in her pocket if she could. You see Daisy is tiny and looks to be part Jack Russell, a reminder of Sarah's loveable dog, Millie, who she has written about. She keeps the group grounded in harmony.

Joanne seems to like all of us too. I think she should rescue a dog, and my mistress would agree. The group counts on Joanne for tweaking of words, attention to detail, and making sure our poetry has some structure, no matter how hard others resist her endeavors. Inspired by Joanne's poetry, everyone in the writing group has taken a turn at poetry. The group has her to thank.

Carole arrives next, and she smells of dog. Her male dog is a little too over-the-top for my taste, but the youngsters seem to like him. Carole could also be named a foody like me. She loves her sweets and always brings enough goodies for an army.

We live with Elizabeth and David in the Storybook House. They rescued us along with many others over the years, as well as fostering thirty-six beagles and beagle mixes. David, our master, who hails originally from England, talks funny but has quite a flair with words. Elizabeth, our mistress, brought us all together, and we, her girls, thank her every day. She is not much for keeping order, but then someone has to try to do it. After all, we are beagles.

After the humans arrive and the pets and fun are over, the work begins. Zoey looks over at Daisy. "Can you believe it? They've spent the last twenty minutes discussing the same word?"

Daisy's white eyelashes make her stare more riveting. "Yeah, they're like a terrier with a bone. They need to adopt some beagle traits—laid back. What do you think Emma?"

"Don't bother me right now. I want to sleep. Wake me when they bring out the food."

Emma

CPSIA information can be obtained
at www.ICGtesting.com
Printed in the USA
BVHW071146250422
635266BV00007B/405